THE LIFE OF A SCREWBALL

Typeset in Minion

Editing, design, typesetting and publishing by UK Book Publishing
www.ukbookpublishing.com

Cover photo: © Nick Hedges

ISBN: 978-1-913179-43-4

THE LIFE OF A SCREWBALL

Stewart Robbins

CHAPTER ONE

Early memories

I GUESS THE EARLIEST MEMORY of my childhood was when I was around five years old. I was living in a caravan, surrounded by farms, and a small airport called Stansted sat a mile across the fields. The caravan was in a place called Takeley in Essex and I lived with my mother, father and two brothers. I should have known back then that my life was going to be different and now, looking back, it would have been more believable if I'd been abducted by aliens.

This was 1963 and a popular way for anyone to earn extra money was to work on the local farms around the area. My mother got a job over the summertime picking potatoes, so she took me along to 'help', like most good parents would! However, being kids we got fed up very quickly! A few of us decided to go and play near a massive crater. Some said it was left by a Second World War bomb; it was full of water, with steep muddy banks and 'Danger Keep Away' signs in full view. This, as we all know in kids' eyes, means 'come and play', plus most of us couldn't yet read. So, in keeping with the tradition of children all over the world, we played. One of the boys said, "this is a German battleship" and threw in an empty tin. Around this hole in the ground were five boys, all aged around five years and two girls about the same age. The boys were dressed in grey shorts, off white tee-shirts and plimsolls, the girls in flower dresses and sandals.

1

We all started rushing around gathering stones and rocks, then stones and rocks rained down, missing the little bobbling bean tin. This went on for about 30 seconds and as the tin didn't sink, I picked up a large concrete rock saying, "blow me, this is heavy, watch this"!

As I went to throw this chunk of concrete, I was too close to the edge and the bloody side of the bank gave way. It must have looked good to the other kids, as I tumbled down, still not letting go (twat), then hitting the water and sinking the tin. One small problem was that I couldn't swim and nobody else could either (I did let go of the rock eventually). I don't know how deep it was, but you never forget the feeling of frizzing water rushing into every open part of your body – I was drowning! Panicked and gasping for air, water flooded in after a few seconds. With every bit of energy I had, I was thrashing around, my arms and legs going in every direction, but I still couldn't keep above the water. Trying to breathe, but sucking in water, a sort of surrender and a cold feeling came over me. It wasn't fear, just blackness, as if I was going to sleep, but no pain.

At that moment in time, the mother and child ESP must have been working, as my mum frantically looked, and I was nowhere in sight. She instinctively ran towards the group of kids looking into the abyss, then she shouted to them "where's Stewart?". My friends, not wanting to get me into trouble replied, "we don't know", but this was not a good time for them to be loyal friends and I guess my mother didn't believed them (as always). As she rushed up to the side of the water's edge, she saw the top of my red hair; she jumped straight in, grabbed my hair and pulled me to the bank. By now, others from all over the fields rushed over to give Mum a hand. I don't really know whether I had stopped breathing or not, but when I think about it now, my heart starts pounding and a feeling of fear come over me. I don't know much about it, but I know my mum gave me the kiss of life, remained cool and calm on the exterior, but was screaming on the inside. Her eyes were blood shot with the look of confusion, a bit of anger and also relief. The farmer came trundling along on his old tractor and flatbed trailer, then I was dumped on the trailer and taken across the fields towards home. Oh, the way to piss your mum off – I said, "Mum, next time do you think Dad could save me?" I don't think the comment went down too well; she looked at me in disbelief, not a spoken word, just the look only a mother can give, and you knew.

As we drove onto the caravan site, some of the local kids were home and it was a novelty seeing me on the back of a tractor, like a carnival trailer and just as my dad arrived home from work too! I remember getting a lecture on the reason why, when parents said don't do something, they mean it. That came as a bit of a surprise, as I always definitely thought it was the other way around.

I was told to go and lie down until the doctor came, a grey haired, thin looking man, about 5′2″ and very well spoken. He gave me a looking over and said to my mum, "He's fine but keep him in quietly for the day." "Impossible," she replied, as living in a caravan came with a set of problems: 32 feet long, 8 feet wide, on wheels with two steps up. Inside the caravan was a bedroom to the rear for Mum and Dad, in the middle was the kitchen and toilet, then at the other end was a dining table, with soft bench seats that turned into a bed for my brothers and me. After the doctor had been and gone, I was told to stay in bed for the rest of the day but that all quickly changed, as my younger brother Mickey was going through a bit of a crisis! In today's environment, you'd have to say he was slightly deranged, and I'd have to agree as it couldn't be explained, it was like something from the modern-day Simpsons!

It all started when he got a second-hand Mickey Mouse front wheel drive tricycle, it was all the rage for up and coming four-year olds. He would take all his clothes off and leave them anywhere on the floor, then just ride off around the site. That boy did not want to keep his clothes on for any reason at all. Every time this happened Mum just went ballistic and shouted "go and find him, Stewart" – she'd go one way, I would go the other, then surely, we'd find him happily riding around without a care in the world, oblivious to everyone around him. We often had people on the site coming to the door with a handful of clothes saying "he's off again". It turned out to be the caravan site's big U.F.O. story: Mick, did he flash around the site on that tricycle. Mickey Mouse having Mickey's naked bum on his face was not good marketing for Disney.

It was the last summer we lived on site, but it was one to remember. A few weeks after I had my first underwater encounter, we were playing at jumping across a small stream and I shouted "me Tarzan" as I landed on the other side. Hiding behind the ditch reeds and shrubs lay waiting for me an old railway sleeper with two rusty 6″ nails sticking out. One of them went through my right shin; I was impaled, I couldn't move.

A few of the boys and girls I was with, jumped over to help me pull my leg off the offending nail and "bloody OUCH" did it hurt. I learnt a new and made up swear word that day! Three of my friends carried me home; on the way back we walked slowly, a good trail of blood dripping along the road was left behind, so it looked like someone had been in a shooting or stabbed (kids' imagination, you can't beat it). We arrived home; Mum just took one look at me and said, "What have you done now?" Her hands on her hips, she was wearing a just below the knee white flowery dress with a blue over-pinny. Mum had this very light long blonde hair and kind vivid blue eyes that would cut right through you when she gave 'that look'. When I told her what had happened she asked if the nail was old and rusty and I replied, "Oh, you know, I had other things on my mind, Mum", while she cleaned the wound with TCP (Ouch Ouch Ouch). What was it about TCP that everyone wanted to use on any cut? I think it was a weapon of control! My friends slipped away as they had seen enough sadistic pain for one day, but then a few hours later they returned with the offending sleeper being dragged along the road. Mum just laughed at the incredible sight! The doctor was called once again and gave me a tetanus jab in the bum. Why the bum!?

It was not long before I was back in trouble again. In the 1960s, Stansted Airport was not so big and was surrounded by broken old World War Two steel open wire fences. These fences were held up by concrete posts every 10 feet, had barbed wire along the top and had a few holes in them. The surrounding area was thick woodland, which went up to the perimeter fence and was without any of the security that you see today. We would often play dangerous games, such as who could get closest to the runway while the planes were landing (nuts, I know). We would lie flat on the grass by the runway and you could feel a rush of air, as the planes landed with the down force moving you along the ground and the noise was deafening. We always knew when we'd been spotted by the pilots, because a few minutes later the security cars based at the flight control tower would start to drive around the airport.

They tried very hard to catch us, but they never did! Once they did get close and this was due to the bird watcher who kept the runway clear of birds, when the planes were taking off or landing. He didn't have too many bird strikes, but he had a shotgun he used to discharge to frighten the birds (and young kids, I think). For some reason we didn't see the Land Rover parked by the runway edge, but he saw us and started to chase us on foot. The three of us split up, two boys ran into the woodlands and I jumped over a two foot retaining wall with a ten foot drop on the other side – "Oh nuts" or "oh shit" possibly, were my first thoughts as I leapt over and realized it was a long drop. As I hit the ground, I heard a horrible crack sound and the feeling I was going to throw up, but as I kept running my arm got bigger and bigger right on the elbow. A broken arm, but I never got caught, though! I can't put into words what was said to me at home.

That day had not been a good day for Mum, as Mick had tried to feed Jerry, my youngest brother, with the contents of his nappy. It was all over Jerry's face, hair and ears but he did have a clean bum. The smell was something that lasted for days, you could taste it in the air. One thing I should point out, nobody ate very much over the next few days and I wonder if it could be used as a dieting method. You could perhaps put it in a bottle and when you feel like eating, just remove the lid.

Our time on the caravan site was brief but I guess they were the times I remember most when I was a child. Things were changing very quickly around me, and we moved to Barking, Essex into my grandmother's three-bedroom terraced house. The front of the house had old dark sooty bricks, it had a well-tended long front garden, slate roof tiles and white sash windows, with white net curtains. My brothers and I all slept in a double bed in the back bedroom, our Uncle Arthur was in the room next to us, Mum and Dad slept in the front room downstairs, and our Nan slept upstairs in the front bedroom. It was tight to say the least – even the dog was fighting for a place to sleep and the cat just gave up and threw himself under a car two days after we moved in!

This was the start of a new chapter in my life, as my childhood had been just like every other kid in the sixties up until this point. At the young age of seven, I was not into flower power or grass, but I did have a crush on Petula Clark! Every time she came onto the black and white television, I would go mad and I don't know why. Then to top it all, I would start crying when the TV programme finished. One of the most traumatic experiences for any kid is a new school, but as I couldn't read or write, to move school at my age was a major problem. This day was looming, 'my first day' and, boy, was I wetting myself. That day was one of the hardest days in my life to date. I can still remember it as clearly as if it were yesterday. When I arrived at school, I was taken to see Mr Woods, the Head Teacher. He was a thin, tall man in his fifties, with brown hair and hair coming out of his long nose. I was nervous to say the least and the first thing he said to me was "oh yes, he looks like a little fireball of trouble". That's the problem with being a redhead, everyone thinks 'trouble'; it's a belief all schoolteachers seem to have in my experience. I was then taken to Miss Harvey's class for assessment; she was a big fat woman, who had horns coming out of her head.

Oh god she was frightening, my heart just started to pound, my ears went pop, and an instant dislike hit me like a train. I could see contempt in her eyes; the first thing she said to me was "you look like trouble, sit at the front of the class so I can keep my eye on you, ginger". When I informed Miss Harvey that I couldn't read or write, she looked at me and said, "I know, I get all the thick kids and troublemakers." One thing was for sure, she had a way of making you feel unwelcome in her class and there was no escape. That was unless you were in the top five, then you were released back in general classes for your age group. She didn't like me one little bit and it was mutual. For a boy to receive such a strong powerful feeling of hatred wasn't good, but I didn't ever tell my mother about the way it was at school. During my first few weeks, I didn't make any friends, I just sat in the playground, just watching the boys play football. Then something changed, I'd really had enough, I was feeling pretty sorry for myself and so I had the hump anyway.

What happened next was out of character for me and I remember it very well. As I walked through the classroom door, into the dragon's den (Miss Harvey's class) the last person always got told off for being last. Guess what, today I was last, and she shouted, "last again", then she slapped me on the back of the head. It made me stumble forwards heading towards a desk, my hands went out to save myself and grabbed a chair to stop me falling over and I gripped onto the solid oak wooden chair. I spun round and threw the chair at her, it bounced off the floor and hit her right on the shin! What a scream that woman let out – "come here, you little bastard" – and she moved bloody quick for a lump of fat. She gave me a crack round the face and boy did that hurt. My ear was ringing, but no way was I going to let her know it hurt, so I just grinned at her. She grabbed me by the hair and started to drag me across the floor to see Mr Woods. I couldn't bear the pain any longer, so in order to make her let go, I grabbed hold of her left arm and sunk my teeth into it. She screamed "let go" and I bit harder! One of us was going to have to give up; I could taste blood by now. Then the classroom doors were opening, and teachers were rushing out to see what all the shouting was about. Teachers came towards us to help her, she let go of my hair and a split second later, I released my bite. We stood looking at each other; the fucking bitch was gripping her arm that was bleeding. You could see in her evil black hearted eyes that she wanted to kill me.

Suddenly I felt a pain across the back of my legs and as I spun around, I saw that Mr Woods had hit me with a three-foot-long bamboo cane. "Get into my office–" his stony face was looking down at me, his eyes were filled with anger –"now, boy". I sat for about thirty minutes, but it felt like hours, just waiting for him to come back to the office. Then finally he burst in and said, "put your hands out" and the stick crashed down onto my hands. First twice on each hand, but when he looked at me and saw no tears, he hit them twice again. It fucking hurt, but I wasn't going to let him see the pain. "Now go and sit outside and wait for your parents." As always it was Mum who came, she wasn't a strong woman emotionally, but when she walked through the door and looked at me, I just cracked and started to cry for about 30 seconds. My mum walked right past me, straight into Mr Woods's office and said, "What have you done to my Stewart?" He told her what had happened and also said "he may be removed from school". Mum just walked out of the office, grabbed my hand and just took me home. She didn't say anything to me at all; it was three weeks before I went back to school – that was cool!

The word had gone around the school, about what I did to Miss Harvey, and for one day, I was someone all the kids wanted to talk to. I was still in the same class and as I walked into the classroom, I looked at Miss Harvey very hard, she frowned at me with her jaw clamped shut. I think she was foaming at the mouth! It was like a scene from a Western, whoever would blink first, would draw their gun, or in our case chalk, board rubbers, books and the little bottles of free milk in the corner of the classroom. That first day back was a war of minds and I could see that she still had a bandage on her big forearm. After that day, an unwritten truce between us seemed to take shape. Basically, she wanted me out of her class, and I wanted to get out, so we worked together to achieve it. I must say, during that first year, I worked the hardest I've ever worked in my whole school life. The old saying 'don't bite the hand that feeds you' did not apply.

One of the problems of being a new boy or girl in school, is getting to know the rest of the kids and for some reason everyone forgets that they were new kids once. We all know the reasons why nobody talks to you; it's because you have the dreaded lurgy, you're dirty or just plain old smelly (plus countless other reasons). It all really boils down to the same thing, you're an outcast for a few weeks, or in some cases throughout your whole school life. In my case, after a few weeks, I started to get a friend or two. Oh yes, the school bully and his friends spotted me, and he got me in the playground, six of them. It's funny that we say school bully, in-fact, bullies are never on their own, are they? The leader has a mouth and a voice that smells as bad as it sounds, rotten, I noticed his teeth were brown. Then you get the hangers on, one is big and thick, and the others seem faceless. I think it's because they are like rats, you know something is there, but you just don't see them. This day they got me with the usual words from the mouthpiece of the gang – "give us your money, or we'll beat the crap out of you". How many times has that phrase been used? I 'm pretty sure they must go on a training course to upgrade themselves on different ways of phrasing it!

Today he was unlucky, I said, "get lost" and I got a smack in the mouth. I didn't see the little shit behind who swung his fist, so I jumped on the boy with all the mouth, who was right in front of me. I'd never been in a fight before, then one of the teachers ran over, pulled me off him and we both got sent to the Headmaster. As we were going up to Mr Woods's office, he must have read his 'three steps to be a better bully' book, as he said, "I will see you outside after school". We both got the cane. I didn't cry, but he did, he howled like a cat and I thought to myself this is the kid that wants to see me after school. Ha, really!

At 4 o'clock we finished school and outside the gates I saw him. "So let's get it over with," I said, as I walked out the school gate. Seven of them were waiting for me and I knew this wasn't going to go well for me. As soon as I came through the black metal rail gate, I immediately went for the same boy again, so at least I'd take one of them out. This kid was the same height, un-brushed hair, looked like a weasel, very scruffy and grimy looking. The look on his face when I lurched myself at him, he just fell back, and I landed on top of him. I don't remember how many punches and kicks rained down on me, but I just would not let go of this little shit. I had him round his throat and I told him to tell them to stop or I would grip harder. To be fair, he couldn't say anything, as I had hold of his throat. It stopped, when his friends saw him turning blue. Then as fast as it started, it stopped, it must have been about 60 seconds. So, I let him up.

He was choking and said, "you're fucking mad" and the rest of them just looked at me with disbelief. I walked on home, blood everywhere, fat lip and a ripped jacket. My mother didn't say a word, just patched me up and I guess she thought that I would deal with it myself. The rest of that year was just hard work in class. Everyone let me be, no more cane, a few more fights, but I started to get on with some of the kids in the playground.

The summer holidays had arrived, six weeks of no school; just what parents all over the country have nightmares about! This was when we got our new council house in Morley Road, Barking. It was a two-bedroom end of terrace, flat-fronted, two up, two down. As you went through the front door, the stairs went up to the first floor, on the left was Mum and Dad's bedroom and straight ahead was the bedroom I shared with my brothers. The toilet was outside, straight in front of you as you opened the back door, in what would be described as a little lean-to. There was no bathroom! The front room had a fireplace and the backroom kitchen had just a butler sink, with a curtain underneath. There was a new boiler, but it was only for hot water. So, with all the mod cons, we moved in. This was great for me; a new house, a new beginning. My grandmother then moved in with my Uncle Arthur, to a new pre-fab house a mile or so away. This was due to redevelopment plans or the factory being extended. After a few days of living there, we started to get to know the other kids on our road. It was a typical road, about 400 yards long, houses on each side of the road and very few cars parked on it. But, halfway along our road was a milk dairy with loads of milk floats parked up. My first real friend was Tony Tribe and he was just as loony as me. The first day I met him, he was sitting on the back of a milk float, just outside the dairy's double green gates.

"What are you doing on the back of that milk float?" I said. He had white bare legs and wore black school plimsolls, no socks, grey shorts and a blue jumper.

"Nothing," he replied; "I was just thinking of taking it for a drive around the block."

"Who said?"

"They did in there, jump on." I thought he was only pulling my leg, as I sat on the back of the empty float. It was electric, had three wheels, one at the front, with a green and white cab bench seat at the front. It suddenly shot forwards about ten feet and Tony passed me on the floor. I'd flown off the back of the float, landing on my bum in someone's front garden. Tony then put his foot down on the starter, fell sideways and fell out of the door.

Nobody even came out to see what the noise was, nobody was hurt, only my belief in Tony's ability to drive. That was the beginning of a very good friendship – but I've never been in a car with Tony driving again to this day! First impressions last for life and then we sat and talked most of the day, until 5 o'clock when the calling came upon us. "Stewart, time to come in for a bath." The bath, a kid's nightmare! I didn't mind the water; it was Mother's washing of my hair that was painful. We all know that it was a way for parents to get their own back on us, the shampoo always got in your eyes, even when you put the flannel over them for protection. I'm sure my mum would soak it in the shampoo first, as whatever you did, it just got in your eyes, which resulted in burning pain and the inability to see for a few seconds, then the drying. It's like your head was put in a food blender, with two sheets of sandpaper, then your body was dried off, using the friction method between two towels. Your skin generates enough heat to dry you and just as you think it's all over, your mum sees a bit of dirt in your ear that even a scientist with a microscope would miss and out comes the cotton wool bud. So, parents, it's not the water, we don't like you bathing us, and god forbid if anyone had paint or any other material on their skin, that wouldn't come off easily. Well, I need not say any more.

We are now in September 1967.

After the bath on this particular night, I sat in the living room with Mum, watching her use the sewing machine. She left the room for a minute saying "don't touch", but I thought a bit of cotton was stuck under the needle. As I put my index finger under it, I stood on the foot control and sewed my skin to the bone. I let out such a scream that my mother thought I was being murdered, there was blood all over the place. "Stewart, I told you to do nothing, you silly little idiot!" Mum had to lift the needle manually from my finger, she cleaned me up with T.C.P. again (ouch) and sent me off to bed. But this day was not over yet. In our bedroom, we had one set of bunk beds, a single bed and we also had . . . a hamster! We'd had him for about three weeks, and he was called 'Mark 2' as 'Mark 1' had already gone missing.

As we didn't have an inside toilet, we had a bucket in our bedroom because the night was too dark. It was used by all of us during the night, so by morning it was generally half full. That night, I forgot to shut the hamster cage and close the lid on the wee bucket. In the morning when got up, he said, "who left the door of the cage open?" and from under the pillow, as I looked at him, he went off: "look Mark 2 is in the wee bucket!" I jumped out of bed and saw poor old Mark 2 floating in the wee bucket. Both Mickey and now Jerry were up, and they were a little upset to say the least. What a way to go – think about it, he gets out from his cage, tastes freedom, then falls three feet into a bucket of pee and drowns. I would rather have been run over or something. That was the last pet we were ever allowed to have in the house. Summer holidays as a kid pass so quickly, but for adults it's not quick enough. This was not a particularly memorable six weeks; we just played in the street. Football only, moving out the way every few hours as a car passed down the road.

I was just nine years old now, getting older but not wiser. The school holidays were over, and I was no longer in Miss Harvey's class, as I'd achieved the required results to move up. I never really saw her much again after that, but I know she was around. During the school holidays, Westbury School had closed down, so the children were all moved into schools around the area and we got most of them. After a few weeks, when everyone had got to know each other, small gangs started to form in the playground and after school, picking on the weak, i.e. kids with glasses, scruffy looking or anything different. We had one black boy called Leroy in our school and we were very good friends.

Outside the playground gates was where most fights would take place and they would just wait for you and then pounce. I was on my way home one day, when one of the gangs were just outside the school gates; five of them pushed Leroy around and just like me, Leroy had never been a fighter. I moved quickly and ran up to them saying "the Headmaster is coming"! They very quickly moved on and I said to Leroy "run, before they notice" and just as I said that, Mr Woods's car pulled out of the school entrance at the other end of the playground. At that moment, I felt a bit windy to say the least, but I said "run" and we were off like rabbits, being chased by a pack of dogs. That description is pretty close, although we didn't look like rabbits. When I finally looked over my shoulder, I could see an ugly pack of boys foaming at the mouth and we'd been just too quick for them and lost them after turning down a few alleys. I walked Leroy home, where his mum, who was a really nice woman, called me ginger top. She was really smiley, with very dark short curly black hair and tall for a woman. She always had a smile. She gave me a drink of lemon water with sugar, before I left. His house was smaller than ours and they had six people living inside.

One of the areas in Barking that was being remodelled was part of the Gas Goring Estate. They were the first two precast tower blocks of their kind. And making way for them, were four rows of houses being demolished. Oh, by the way, there was no health and safety, just wide-open houses being stripped out and prepared to be knocked down. Anyone could go inside them and if you can imagine this in your mind's eye, think of a film where a bomb had gone off and debris was left all over the road. There were little bonfires of roof timbers and other burning timber, generating black smoke and left to burn out on the roads that were covered with bricks and window frames. The demolition lads all looked the same: flat caps, dirty faces, hands like shovels and arms like gorillas. Hanging around and working, breathing in all the shit, but that didn't matter, as they smoked Golden Virginia roll-ups to keep the dust out of their lungs!

On the way home, I walked across this demolition site – bad move, as I had forgotten that was the area where most of the gangs hang out. I walked right into the lot that were chasing me, but there were now ten of them. As I said before, gangs are the same the world over. The Leader is often the smallest one with all the mouth, a big dumb one or fatty the enforcer, then the rest of them who didn't pass nappy training are faceless. I didn't let them say much to me – I knew I was going to get a good kicking – so I just charged towards the bossy one. His face had 'oh shit' written all over it, as I hit him head on into his chest like a rugby tackle. As we hit the ground, my hands were still around him and I felt all the skin come off my knuckles. We hit the ground with my full weight on top of him, it knocked the wind straight out of him, and he started to cry. His mates tried to pull me off him, but the harder they tried the tighter my grip got; they punched, kicked, pulled my hair and even bit my arm. When a security guard with a dog saw us, he shouted "you lot, piss off, or I will let the dog go". With that, everyone just stopped what they were doing and ran like the clappers, but as I got off the floor, the guard let the dog off its lead. I didn't stop to think about the other kid on the ground, as that dog looked straight at me – I know it sounds daft, as the guard was about a hundred yards away, but that big ugly dog had a Stewart-seeking nose!

I ran into an old house and as I ran up the stairs, I heard the guard shout "Rex", then the mutt turned around, stopped and then started to walk away, as he looked back at me looking out of the upstairs window. I'm sure he had a grin on his face, while he lifted his leg and peed all over my school bag that I'd dropped on the floor. It was not a good day for me as, when I came down the old stairs, one of the steps gave way, I went head over heels and hit every step on the way down. Bang, crash, bump! As I hit the bottom of the landing, my hand tried to grab something to stop me falling further. For a few seconds I just lay on the floor, going over my body in my mind, to see if all my parts were all there! My hand was throbbing and slowly I lifted my right hand to look at it. Blood was pumping out and down my arm, the gash on my palm was about two inches long. I didn't think about the blood; just what Mum was going to say to me when I got home.

I dragged myself up off the bottom of the stairs, picked up my bag and started to walk. Some people walked past and looked at me, but not one person said a thing. Things are no different today, people just don't want to get involved unless it suits them. I was a young boy bleeding, the right arm of my shirt was covered in blood, and as I walked up to the front Mum saw me through the window; she opened the door and with a big sight and said, "Stewart, what have you done now?". As soon as she spoke to me, I burst into tears. This is something a lot of kids seem to do, they can be in bad pain, yet hold it in until they think it's safe to let it out. It's not only kids that hold pain in, we have all seen both men and women do it in various ways. The most common is when somebody hurts themselves or stubs their toe, they hum a little song and do a little jig around the room, looking round to see who is in earshot of them. The rest I will leave to your imagination. "Stop crying," she said, "it's only a small cut, it just looks bad because of all the blood everywhere." Mum cleaned the wound up, then took me to hospital for stitches.

When we arrived at Old Church Hospital, a big gorilla wearing a dark blue uniform greeted us. Matron said, "What has the little terror been up to?" So Mum explained, and she looked at me and grunted, which I took to mean 'come with me to see the doctor'. You know, I swore her knuckles dragged along the ground as she walked. You did not have much of a wait to see the doctor then, and he turned out to be a tall, softly spoken, tanned, thin man with jet black hair, and he was wearing a very white coat. "We need to give you a few stitches," he said, and I felt all the blood drain from my body. Then came the immortal words "be a brave little boy, it won't hurt" (forgive me if I don't believe it). I was right, it was like having your teeth drilled without any painkilling injections. The gorilla (Matron) told me, "Stay still, lie down on the bed and be a good boy for the doctor." Then they put a freezing spray on my hand and out came the tool, a curved needle about two inches long. As he drove it into my hand, I jumped up into the air. "Matron," said the doctor, "hold him down." The nurse grunted, "Don't be a big baby." I could see she was enjoying this moment; her face had a big smirk and every time I felt the needle stab into my hand, it hurt me so much I thought I was going to faint! After five stitches I looked at Mum, hoping she would stop the pain and it was finally over. The doctor cleaned the wound, the bitch let me go and said, "That was not too bad after all, was it?" I looked at her and said, "I didn't feel a thing", with tears streaming down my face.

On the way home I said to Mum, I was so sorry for cutting myself and I would try to stay injury free. She looked at me with a warm smile and said, "Well, Stewart" (or most of the time Mum called me 'screwball') "somehow, I just don't think that's possible where you're concerned, do you?" Maybe mothers have an insight into our hidden depths, or they just know us so well. "Is everything all right at school?" "Yes."

The next morning, walking through the school gates about 8.45am, I saw the same gang I'd had a punch up with the night before; they were standing by the toilets, just inside the main gates. The toilets were an old WW2 bomb shelter, constructed from with a concrete roof, 9-inch dark yellow stock brick walls and at each end were the entrances, one for girls and one for boys. They were trying to look tough, with lolly-pop sticks in their mouths! I don't know what got into me, I just started walking towards them, I felt an inner rage and red mist come over me, then I heard a voice calling me from behind, and I stopped in my tracks. When I turned my head, it was Leroy. "Stewart, leave it, don't waste your time." It took the red mist away, so I turned and walked towards the main playground. The play area was a walled off part of the school, about half the size of a football pitch, girls and boys doing everything, football, hop skip jump, kiss chase, and British Bull Dog. At 9.00am, a teacher would blow the whistle, and everyone would file off upstairs to the Assembly Hall. School uniform for the boys was grey shorts, jumpers and socks, with a white polo shirt. The girls wore grey skirts and jumpers, with a white polo shirt and socks.

After a few days, most of the bullies and gangs had found other kids to pick on, or rival gangs from other schools, as I was too much trouble.

I was now ten years old and in my last year at this school. This was a good time, with no problems, and the construction site opposite the school was taking shape. On weekends, Tony and I would work for the bricklayers, making the tea and coffee, or sweeping up. We would get Half a Crown, or Fifty Pence in today's money. It was good for a few months during the warm weather, up until mid-June, and most of us would then go swimming at the local pool, which was about five hundred yards away. Most of the bricklayers would go to it at the end of the day, instead of having a bath! It was an indoor pool and all the lads and us would jump off the high boards, bombing each other. You can't do that now – all good things come to an end! Now the site had reached an end, all four Bison tower blocks were finished.

So, once the next school half term was upon us, Tony and I would just go and play around Barking Creek. This was a hub of activity, factories along the river, with barges and small tugs chuffing up and down. This was a Tuesday evening around four o'clock, we were just walking along the riverbank, the tide was low and it was a nice sunny day. My arm just shot up in the air and I felt a sudden burning pain in my right hand, I lost my footing and fell down the riverbank into the silt and dark blue mud. Tony jumped down the bank and grabbed me. "What happened?" We were both covered in stinking river black mud. "I don't know, my right hand is hurting me–" and I scrambled back up the riverbank, using one hand with Tony's help. "Look at your hand," he said and embedded in the centre of my hand was a piece of lead, with blood all around it. I just pulled the lead out and started to jump up and down in pain, as the penny dropped: I had been shot!

We continued to walk home and as my hand was bleeding and burning in pain, it was hard not to cry. As we got to the bottom of the road, Tony spotted a light blue and white police car, with a Ford Anglia police sign on top; it had a blue light planted on top like a beacon and it was parked on a side road close to the river bank. Tony ran up to the two officers sitting having lunch. "What's up, lads?" and I showed them my hand, saying it was hurt and asked if they could help.

One of the officers, a big stocky plump man, with long black bushy sideburns, got out of the car and walking round to me asked, "What happened to you, ginger, what trouble have you been getting yourself into then?" When I told him, he said, "hold on here a minute", and he walked back to his partner who was still eating something in the car, who then handed the first aid box through the window. "Call an ambulance," said the constable and after a few minutes I could hear police cars coming from all over the place. I heard the Officer say to his Sergeant on the radio," young lad's been shot" and just then an Officer with all the pips on his shoulder pulled up in an unmarked black Rover 90. He came over wanting to know what had happened and as I was telling him the story, another of the Officers on the riverbank wall, let out a shout to his colleagues and they all started to run towards the steep grass-covered bank, to the concrete two feet high retaining wall along the edge of the river. At the end of the road, another two police cars sped off to the other side of the riverbank.

After about 20 minutes or so, they all returned, and they had someone with them. He was a small, light mousey haired male, about thirty years old, very slim, wearing stained jeans, black jacket, a whitish vest and had tattoos of crosses on his hands. One of the Officers was carrying a rifle, which he gave to the Senior Officer in charge. This man started kicking off a bit, so he was hit with a brown wooden truncheon that was about a foot long. You could hear a flat thud on his head, then blood instantly washed down his face over his eyes and dripped off his chin, then two of the police picked him up like he was a piece of meat and threw him into the back of the black van, while shouting something that I couldn't make out.

The ambulance took me to hospital; good news, they didn't give me any stitches this time. Tony and I were then taken home in a police car, which was great! The Officer said, "Would you like me to put the blue lights on when we go down your road?" "Yes please!" All the kids in the street were looking and people came out into the street to see what the problem was. When we reached my front door, Mum was already waiting by the front gate, with the Officer who had all the pips. He informed her what had happened. Mum looked at me and her eyes just rolled, as she put her arms around me and said, "You will be the death of me one day, Stewart".

Everyone at school wanted to know what had happened to me; I let them make up their own minds. Silly things were being said like 'it was the Krays' or 'the Mafia' and one off the wall one was, 'it was a hit gang' put out on me. Mind you, you never know what you can buy with a Sherbet Dip or an Ice Jubbly! This lad did get a funny sideways look, as we all carried on talking about it. After that day, it was old news in the playground, and everything went back to normal. My fifteen minutes!

Over the next few months, I was getting into more and more fights every day. Mum was getting fed up with cleaning and repairing me, so one day she pulled me to one side and asked, "Stewart, do you win any of your fights at school? You have some mean black eyes; I'm going call you panda."

"How can I, when most of the time it's four or five kids getting me!" I was very popular! "Tell me what happens . . ." "It always starts in the play-ground, I see the bully boys picking on other kids, so I go over and try to stop them, they go away, wait outside school for me and then it's a free for all." It was becoming like the Roman Gladiators, every night the kids would wait around outside school just to see if I had a fight that night.

Most fights would only last a few minutes, because I always went for the nose and once blood appeared, it seemed to scare off some of the kids I was fighting. I was still getting a good kicking; you cannot fight four or five against one and hope to win very often, let me tell you! Mum told me that she used to get into a lot of punch ups, when she was a kid; she was a bit of a tomboy and didn't play with her sisters, only with her brother Arthur. "I will give you some advice, Stewart, the next time you get into trouble, find a wall, put your back up against it and then they can only come at you from the front. People think twice, if they can only come at you from the front." It wasn't very long before I put this into use. She also showed me how to box, get my hands up and hold your fist tight, punch to the nose, hit the tummy, attack first, look at their eyes, as they will tell you where they're going to try and hit you. We had a few fun fights in the garden over a few nights. I also think Mum got a few hits in on me, for past – let's say – discrepancies!

It was a strange day; as I left for school, Mum said, "see you later" and I didn't think any more about it until much later. In class, the girl that was sitting behind me was the sister of the gang leader, she played on it telling everyone that if they didn't do everything she said, her brother would beat the life out of them (to say the least). This never bothered me until today, when she said to the smaller girl next to her, "I see you have a chocolate, Milky Way, give it to me, or I will tell my brother and he will take it off you." At this point I turned around and said, "I will flatten your brother." She looked at me with a face that would melt snow, but as I turned back, I felt a stabbing pain in the centre of my back. I let out a yell jumping up. "The little bitch has stabbed me with her ink pen." The teacher didn't even come over, he just sent us to the Headmaster's Office. As we walked to the Head's room across the Assembly Hall I said, "I'm not going to hit you, but I will get your brother for this." She said, "piss off", very lady like. We both got told off and sent back to class. At the end of the day word had gone around that I was going to fight someone outside the playground tonight, so about 30-plus kids of all ages from school were waiting for me. This little gang, its jumped up leader and his six hench boys were all looking at me, as I walked through the main school gate. Inside my head, my Mum's voice popped up, straight to the wall it said. I put my back up against the nearest wall, as two of them came at me.

I hit one of them right on top of his nose – Mum said always go for the nose, it takes the high ground, it's very painful and puts them off for a few seconds. It was a sweet hit, I felt it crack splat, he started to scream out loud and the other kid backed off. The rest of the gang looked at the one who seemed to be in charge, who said, "let's all get him" and I thought my number was up. Just then, Mum appeared through the crowd of kids, grabbed the gobby one by the scruff of his jumper and said, "let's make it fair, shall we. You fight him, big boy, by yourself"! The other kids stood back. Bruce was the boy's name, he looked very unsure, so I shot off the wall straight at him and I hit him with a right forearm smash to the face, he hit the ground with a thud, I jumped on top of him, but when he started to cry I stopped. I could hear all the kids around me shouting 'hit him, hit him'. So, I left the sad twit on the floor, but as I was getting up someone slapped me around the back of the head saying, "get up, boy, you're a bully".

At that moment my mother pushed through the crowd and grabbed hold of the person dragging him off. The kids started to laugh, because it was a teacher that my mum had pulled off me. The teacher's face went as white as a sheet, with a look of shock, as he stumbled backwards while protesting loudly. I could see Mum wagging her finger at him, as he stood like a small kid being told off. I didn't hear what was said, but he could not get a word in. Mum turned and just left him standing there, she came over, grabbed me and we walked off; after that everyone went home. I didn't have any more fights at that school, nobody picked on me again, but I was never one for mixing with others and I never played Kiss, Chase or Bulldog and girls just didn't like me – it must have been the red hair! As we walked home, I said, "Mum, why can't I make friends, I try, and nobody seems to like me at school?" She put her hand on the back of my neck and with a smile said,

"I don't like you, so why should anyone else?" What? She smiled at me and said, "I'll race you home." Mum could run. It was about 100 metres to the front door and she shot off. I couldn't get anywhere near her at all.

She called me screwball – I think she should look at herself! It was my birthday in a few weeks and Mum asked if I would like a party. I'd never had a party before, and I said yes. "Let's get all the invites made, give them out and get an answer as you hand them out."

So, I went up and down the street and got 10 yeses. Steven and Tony said yes plus others. The night before, Mum was up late, and I helped with making the cakes and stuff for the party. I was so excited I was bursting inside. I couldn't sleep on Friday night; the party was the very next day. I was up in the morning, and 12 o'clock was the time for everyone to come around. Mum had made some hats, we had sweets, everyone was going to get a jamboree bag (this was a bag with mixed sweets, Black Jacks, Bubble Gum, Flying Saucers, little sweet cigarettes and sherbet dips, plus if you were really lucky a Gob stopper that would last a week). I was looking out the front window from about 11 o'clock. Mum set the table with the juice, a blue icing-covered cake, with candles and she'd also made little triangle fish paste sandwiches.

It was now 12.30pm and no one had arrived so far. Mum asked if I'd told them the time, yes, I was sure I did. My brothers kept asking if they could start eating yet and got the response "no, wait". It got to about 1 o'clock and Mum just went, "let's eat, shall we". I sat there in the front room feeling very sorry for myself, I really wanted to cry at that moment – not even Tony and Steven came – my best friends. So, Mum came and sat next to me, put her arm around me and said this: "Only family matters, Stewart, only family and we are your family, so let's enjoy your day, have some fun in the garden." Mum was just about to start lighting the candles when Tony and Steven came to the back door. "Hi Stew, sorry our mums took us to the other party in Keith Road. . ." "What party?" my mum said. "A wedding party at someone's house, everyone is there, but we wanted to come here, so we bunked off."

Mum had a face like thunder, but they weren't looking at Mum when they saw the food on the table. "Well come in then, come on then" and they ate everything in sight. Mum and the boys all gave me the bumps in the garden, we played with the home-made crossbows, made by my mum and they were really good. Two sticks tied together like a cross, a wooden peg with two small nails each side and a strong elastic band. Paper targets with pictures – I think of the other parents! It was a good day, but one that has haunted me all my life. I will never again put myself in that situation of vulnerability to others – no more parties. It was very, very unusual to see Mum angry and the next day I know Mum went around and gave a piece of her mind to a few people over this situation. Mum was a very kind soul, but this was too much. They knew this party was coming up, so they could have said something and we would have moved it to Sunday. Mum knew it affected me badly, very badly. In fact, I never ate anything at all, I was not feeling up for it, it had been killed at the start. Sunday we always had a roast, but the only meat we could afford was rabbit. With lots of green 'yuck', roast potatoes and Mum would sometimes make Jam roly-poly with powder tasting custard. We loved it! I was always looking forward to Mum's cooking, she was great, but if you ever went around to Nan's, my god you would die from cholesterol poisoning. First, we would be given a sugar sandwich on white bread, or dripping spread, but she did make a mean Bread Pudding.

Now I was going to be 11 next year and I was going up to the next school. Mum said Joan and Pete needed me to babysit this Sunday evening, because they were out to a party. This night was a little different to normal: Joan and Pete never came home, because they got so drunk, they fell asleep on the train and ended up in Birmingham. Mum had to feed Joan and Pete's kids too. Joan and Pete turned up at midday looking rocked and apologised to Mum and Dad. I got 10 pounds! Mum and Dad seemed to be a bit frosty over something that had happened the weekend before. What happened was, we'd all been out as a family and went around to Dad's brother's for a Sunday lunch. When we arrived, Mike (Dad's brother) was outside with his new American red convertible Mustang.

Everyone was looking at it, Mick and I absolutely loved it, it was great. I was trying to get in it and Mike told me to keep out of it. Mum and

Dad went inside, then Jerry and Mickey were allowed to get in the car. I wasn't fussed! Then Don (Dad's other brother) came out of the house saying, "shall we go for a ride then, everyone" and I immediately said yes. "Oh, Stewart, before we go, can you go to the shop for me and pick up the Sunday papers, no need for any money just say Mike sent you. Hurry so we can go." I ran as quickly as I could, I wanted to get back for this ride in the cool car, but when I got to the shop which was 300 yards away, it was closed. Then, as I started back, they drove right past me with Mickey waving to me. I thought oh well, I'll get a chance when I get back. So, I went in see Mum and she asked where Mick and Jerry had gone. "Out in the new car," I said. "Did you not want to go?" I said "yes". So, I told her what had happened, and she went outside to see if Mike and Don were back yet. They were gone for a long time and when Mike and Don finally got back, it was time for dinner. Then after dinner, Dad went out in the car with his dad. I was still hoping to get out for a ride, but as soon as they arrived, Mike said that's it now, there's no more petrol, sorry. I felt a little left out and Mum asked Dad why did Stewart not get to go. He told her it was because I didn't want to and when I went to the shop, I was gone for a long time. Also, during the conversation, Mum started talking about past Christmases. She said the strangest thing, again I didn't understand what they were on about, but this is what I could hear. "You know they don't show any interest in him; they treat him like a leper. Last Christmas they got him nothing, the others got lots of stuff and we took some of it and hid it away, so that it did not look so bad. Talk to them, Len, or I will." He told Mum, that's the way they were, but he would talk to them. Maybe one day it will fall into place, who were they talking about?

It was getting a bit heated, but it was time for bed. As I went to bed, only Mum just said goodnight to me, Dad did his usual and never said a word. Mickey and Jerry just kissed Dad and Mum, and we went up. I could still hear them talking loudly for hours; well it felt like hours and I drifted off.

CHAPTER TWO

Life changing moment

IT WAS LATE JUNE 1967, it got light about 5 o'clock in the morning, it was wet and windy – the order of the day. On this Friday, about 7.00am and half asleep, I came downstairs where Mum and Dad were having a row. I didn't understand what it was about, but I think it was still going on from other day. I caught the last bit she said as he left – "why don't you drop dead" – he slammed the door on his way out, never even gave me a second look, got into his friend's car and went to work. Mum was still red eyed and upset when I left for school later that morning. On Fridays after school, a few of us always went swimming at Barking indoor swimming baths. Tony and I now had a new addition to our small two-person gang, it was Steven who'd just moved into our road. He was a tall scrawny lad, with yellow teeth, that were like a row of bombed houses, or tombstones. His breath would kill a fly from 20 feet! All day was a very strange day, you know when you have a premonition, a feeling something wasn't right.

Today was this sort of day, I felt very strange, something was wrong. Walking home from swimming as always, we were hungry, it was about 6pm, so we stopped off and bought some chips and crackling served in newspaper, lots of salt and vinegar (using our bus fare to pay for it). We carried on walking home, eating them from the newspaper. On the way, we passed two police officers walking, one with his hands behind his back, talking to a WPC. I looked at them and for some reason I wanted to ask them something, but why I felt that I wasn't sure – ask them what? I kept looking back, they must have thought we were guilty of something – most of the time we were! Something about them I didn't like, and what I was feeling was butterflies.

Tony said, "What's a matter?"

"I don't know," I said, as we turned into our road. I looked back again to see if the two officers were coming around the corner – no. I felt a bit of relief, though I still couldn't put my finger on it. "See you tomorrow, mate." As kids we never went through the front door, always round the back of the house, to use the toilet first or just in the back door, never through the front. We had no lights in the old bog – for that, you'd need a bit more upmarket toilet. We did have posh toilet paper though, it was white and a little rough, not like the bloody tracing paper at school. I used it, flushed the chain and went in through the back door. The same two officers that we'd passed earlier were in the front room and Mum was crying. Then there was a knock at the door, the WPC opened it and my Uncle Don (Dad's brother) came in followed by his wife.

"Mum what is going on?" But no one took any notice of me at all – it was as if I was looking out of a goldfish bowl.

Mum and Don then left the house with the officers. I was really mystified now, but our Aunt Doreen said, "Your dad has been in a car crash and your mother has gone to see him in hospital." I understood now, but my two younger brothers were confused, still trying to watch the TV. I stayed up as late as I could to wait for Mum to come home, but I fell asleep in the armchair.

I woke in the morning, my mother's coat was lying across me and she was sitting opposite talking to Doreen – her eyes puffy, full of pain and red.

"Mum, what has happened to Dad?" I asked.

"Your father has been in a car crash, he is in a coma."

"What's a coma?"

"He's in a deep sleep." And she started to cry. "It's my entire fault," she said, "if I hadn't shouted at him and said, "drop dead" this wouldn't have happened."

Doreen said, "Nobody could have stopped that crash, Len was a passenger, not the driver and if it's anyone's fault, it was the driver's, for driving too fast." What had happened was, Dad and two others were coming home from work in Mike's Mini, (Mike was Dad's best friend). As they passed over a railway bridge in London, they lost control on an oil spill that hadn't been cleaned up from a previous accident, they spun off and hit one of the supports to the passenger's side. Dad was thrown out of the front windscreen and hit the bridge, causing extensive head injuries. Everyone else in the car was only slightly injured; fortunately, Dad wasn't wearing a seat belt, because if he had been, he'd have been killed instantly as the front wing had folded over onto the front passenger seat. I wasn't fully sure what was going on, I knew that my dad was not dead, but I also knew that my mum needed me to be the head of the house. She never actually said it, I just knew that is what she wanted – I took it as read anyway. Every day for three months, Mum would pack me off to school and then catch the hospital bus, to sit at Dad's side, while he was in a coma. She kept a daily diary and Mum would take my brothers to Aunt Doreen, for them to be looked after, but I never went there! Mum would be home when I got in from school, and at weekends, I would go down to Peter and Joan's who lived at the end of our road, about 10 doors away. My brothers were always with Dad's brothers or aunties while I would be babysitting the three kids, Martin 3, Gary 5 and Debbie 2, as they always went out on Friday and Saturday nights. I'd just turned ten and was now a babysitter – how times had changed!

On Saturday they would go to the Workingmen's Club and come home about 12ish, with lots of their well lubricated friends, who would continue with more drink till about four in the morning, dancing, chatting, and I would just watch and enjoy the happy laughter and drunken comments, plus I would always get a few tips for being the one going off and getting people a drink from the back room. I knew how to open a Party Seven, without it going all over the place – note: for those of you who do not know what a Party Seven is, it's seven pints of beer in one big tin. To open it, you would have to use an opener that was about 4 inches long, an inch wide and a pointed end with a little hooking piece to catch the rim for leverage. If you got it wrong, you got covered in beer from the spray. I did that a few times: always two holes. I was also mixing drinks, Bacardi and Coke, Rum and Black, Gin and Tonic, Martini, the list went on, but you get the point. Joan and Peter's house was a little bigger than ours, with three bedrooms. It also meant that Mum got some time to put her feet up, as Jerry and Mickey were with Grandmother and Grandfather. I never understood why they spent so much time with them, as I didn't feel such a connection to them. They never seemed to speak much to me – anyway quite cool with me.

It was Saturday evening; I was watching the black and white TV with the push buttons on the set itself. Only three channels: BBC1, BBC2 and ITV – from Radio Rentals – we, like everyone else, rented our TV. I can't remember what we were watching, but around this time usually it would have been Z Cars, Ironside, Bewitched, or it could have been The Beverly Hillbillies. I think it was just me and Mum, as Mickey and Jerry were with Don and Doreen out visiting some place. It was about 7pm, there was a knock at the front door, and it was Mike, Dad's best friend, who had been driving the car in the accident. Mum gave him a hug. He looked so grey and sad, his whole demeanour was of remorse. He told Mum he was so, so sorry, his eyes red, full of confusion and tears.

"It's not your fault," Mum said.

He started to cry (a grown man) – it was the first time I had seen a man cry. I thought that once you reached 10, that was it, you were indestructible, and men don't cry. Girls and Mums always cry, that was the way we all thought life was.

They went into the kitchen to talk more, then there was a loud thumping sound on the front door, as if someone was in a panic. When I opened the door, it was Don and Mike (Dad's brothers), they pushed me aside, as if I wasn't there, then they started to shout at Mike in the kitchen. "It's your fault Len is in hospital; you are the one who should be in there."

27

Mum jumped in and screamed "shut up, it was an accident". I ran out of the house to knock at Peter and Joan's house, and Peter came to the door. "Son." Pete was 6 feet, 3 inches tall, built like a tank and was an East End bear knuckle fighter! He was always wearing a white vest at home, baggy bottoms and flip flops, and had an oil slick of brushed back, jet black hair. I told him what was going on and he called back to Joan "just popping out" and closed his front door. We headed off to my house and got there just in time, before it got ugly as Mum was shouting and crying. Pete just walked in and told Don and Mike to "leave now". They looked at him and said, "piss off, it's none of your business". Pete was not a person you would say that to and expect to keep your teeth. Don and Mike were both also about 6′1″, but still no match for Pete. "Yes, it is," he replied in a very deep cool voice, "fuck off", his hand clenched, with his thumb sticking out and pointing over his shoulder towards the open front door. "Or, I'll throw you out." And for a split second it looked like they were going to try their luck with Pete, but they backed down.

As they left, Mike turned back and said, "Our brother made a mistake meeting you and your bastard son!" Pete spun around and punched him so hard in the face, a dull thud lifted his feet off the ground. He lay on his back, moaning on the floor, Pete grabbed Don and pushed him through the open front door, he picked up Mike, who was bleeding from his eye and mouth, shoved him out and slowly closed the door on them without saying another word. After about ten minutes, Mum had stopped crying and Dad's best friend left. With Peter as bodyguard, Mum and I were alone now, the house was very still, the TV was off, but as she went to say something to me, there was another knock at the door. It was my Uncle Fred, who had come round to see Mum. She said that he could take me out on Sunday afternoon. "OK," he said, "I'll meet him outside the Barking Town Hall." He was about 5′8″, a stocky ginger haired man and was a Naval officer of some kind. He was always very smartly dressed, like he had just come out of a steam press. Sometimes, I would go out with my uncle, often he would take me to the zoo or the pictures, but most of the time he wouldn't turn up! I would be sitting around waiting for him. When we got back home, he said bye and left without even coming into the house or asking why Mum looked so puffed in the face. At the time, I thought he was related to one of my aunts, I never put two and two together.

"Stewart, would you like to come and see your dad, now it's the Easter Half Term?"

"Yes."

"Ok, don't tell your brothers, because they'll get upset."

It was Monday morning and I got up very early, the boys were going out with Dad's family for the day. We left home about 10am, got on the red double decker route master, with a conductor who collected the money and gave us a ticket. It was three bus changes to get to the Woolwich Ferry, then we crossed on the ferry to the Woolwich Hospital. Mum knew the way, as she had visited so many times. When we got to the ward, I saw it had cream walls, with white metal tube beds each side of the ward (which was about 70 feet long). This was a 'men only' ward, the patients were all sitting up, with their visitors seated around them on little green plastic stacking chairs. Dad was at the far end of the ward, on the right-hand side, next to a window. I remember the ward had high ceilings, with light grey vinyl flooring and smelt of hospital. It had taken us three hours to get there, it was now about 1pm and visiting times were very strict – we had till 3pm. A very nice smart nurse, with a dark blue uniform, a small white hat sitting on top of her hair like a chimney and a red belt with a silver buckle made a beeline for us. She said, "Hello Mrs Byrne, Mr Byrne woke up last night, but before you see him, could you speak to the doctor."

She showed us into this dimly lit room, where we waited for the doctor until he arrived in a very white coat and a stethoscope around his neck. I had no clue what was being said, but he informed her that there was some brain damage and that they wouldn't be able to tell how bad it was for a few weeks. Mum said she had been warned of that before. I was not interested in what was being said, I just wanted to see my dad for the first time in months, I felt full of joy and I wanted to tell him all about school and things. When we got to his closed curtain, my heart started to pump with excitement, but that was very short lived, as when I saw my dad, I didn't recognize him. I wanted to run away, thinking this is not my dad, we're in the wrong place, but I just stood frozen to the spot looking at him and I had a lump in my throat. My eyes welled up. Dad had an air tube coming out of the centre of his neck and one out of his nose, with two drips going into his arm. His face was black and blue, and his head was shaven, with stitches to his forehead. He was making a groaning sound, as Mum brushed her hand across his shaved head saying, "everything will be alright, Len, Stewart is here to see you." No movement or sound came from him. Mum kissed him on the side of the forehead and said, "I love you; don't you give up, Len" and standing by the bedside, I wanted to touch him, I felt I needed to. My hand lay on top of his hand. A sad feeling of loss and confusion came over me. "It's time to go now, Stewart." The time had gone so quickly. On the ferry home, I asked if I could go again in a few weeks, but I didn't get a response. She smiled at me and slid her hand over the top of my head, to the back of my neck and said, "Stewart, we all have to be brave, there are hard times ahead."

I knew then that my mother needed my help with everything, so I started to not go to school. I would bunk off and go home using the back door that was never locked, to be there waiting for her, when she came back from the hospital. This went on for a few weeks, until the school sent round an Inspector to speak to Mum. She was a little upset to say the least, in fact she was so pissed off, I was grounded for six weeks. So, if that was not bad enough, a boy of my age being taken to school by his mum was just wrong in all the other kids' eyes! Things were about to get even worse; Mum never believed that a good smack worked every time, she would have alternative ways, but being stuck indoors for weeks and having to come home from school and not go out to play, was driving me nuts. Talking to my mates out of the bedroom window at night was not good at all, my street credibility had totally gone! It was Thursday night – oh yes on weekends I was allowed out – just not school nights. I was playing darts in the back room, we had the dart board on the back door that led to the outside bog, or toilet if you were posh. Mum said, "put the darts down, Stewart, before someone gets hurt, your younger brothers are running around" and to be fair, they were running in and out of the garden through the back door.

"Can I have one more go, Mum?"

"No."

So, in a defiant tantrum I turned around with all three darts in my hand and threw them towards the dartboard. Mickey opened the back door, at that right or wrong moment, and one of the darts went straight into his forehead. He let out a scream that would shatter glass.

Mum rushed into the back room and grabbed Mickey, who was looking like a Dalek from Doctor Who. Mickey was just frozen to the spot, balling his eyes out and Mum removed the dart, but he just kept sobbing his little heart out. She said, "I told you to put the darts away and because you didn't do as you were told this has happened." I was expecting to get a good hiding but instead was told "get to bed, now". The next morning Mum still didn't say much to me and that was never a good sign, but she also had a look in her eyes that made me feel very uneasy. I was not sure what to expect!

I and most kids like to get things out of the way, get a good smack and it's over with, but this time nothing happened. Friday morning, as we got to the school gates I said, "see you tonight" and Mum said, "hold on, Stewart, I'm going to take you into the playground". "No, Mum, please no, no." She grabbed my arm – "come on" – as she frog-marched me into the playground and all the kids watched us. This was my hard kid reputation out of the window – it had taken years to build and it was now going down the pan. Then she said, "I need to go now", kissed me on the cheek and gave me a hug. I just wished a big hole would open up and swallow me, she whispered "did I do something you didn't want me to do?", then she walked out the gates leaving me gobsmacked, red faced and looking at the ground! I think I got the message; my leg was pulled all day, little shouts from girls "Mummy's boy", as they were the only ones that could get away with it – the boys just gave a knowing grin, while thinking, thank god that wasn't me!

A few weeks had gone by, not a lot happened at home, Mum was still going to the hospital to see Dad. My curfew was over after a week, as Mum had got fed up with me being under her feet. Then Mum walked through the door after a hospital visit and told us "your Dad will be home soon".

"When?" "Possibly Monday." This was in three days. "If the doctor passes him fit enough." I could not wait till Monday, I was bursting at the seams to see him, every day I was "is Dad going to be home on Monday?" "yes, he will", but I could see Mum wasn't right, she didn't have that smile when we all knew she was happy (maybe it was the apprehension of him coming home). All of Sunday night I couldn't sleep, I was like a cat on a hot tin roof. I was allowed to take the day off school to see Dad come home; Dad's brother Don took Mum in his car to go and fetch him from hospital and I kept looking out of the window to see when they were coming back. My brothers were playing out in the back garden and I don't remember them missing Dad – I guess at the time they were too young. They knew he was ill in hospital, but I guess when you're too young to understand, you are easily distracted. I was watching from my mum's bedroom and saw Don's car come round the corner. I was making sure I looked smart for my dad, I put on my best shorts and even cleaned my shoes, my hair was also brushed and that was a first for me! I rushed downstairs shouting "they're here" opening the door for them. Don and Mum had Dad between them, as they walked through the door; he was still a bit weak and he had a white dressing gown around his throat. I was standing with a big smile on my face, I said "Dad", but he just looked at me. Something was wrong. I felt very unsure at that moment, they moved past me as I moved out of the way and I closed the door behind them. They sat him down in the armchair and Mum went into the kitchen to make tea for everyone, while I stood by the front door for some time, thinking that my Dad still wasn't well, but he would speak to me soon.

Then Mickey and Jerry came in from the garden, and as they walked into the room and saw Dad, he put out his arms. As they went over to him, he held them, he couldn't speak very well because the hole in his neck was still healing, but he was saying something to my brothers, but I couldn't hear what. As Mum came into the room with the tea, she saw the boys sitting with Dad and saw me standing by the door, she said, "Stewart, come over and see your Dad", but as I started to walk towards him he said something else that I couldn't make out. It was clear that Mum must have, though, as she then said "Stewart, will you get me the other cups of tea from the kitchen?". I felt that I wanted to burst into tears, I was feeling so very sad inside, and as I walked to the back of the house to get the cups my brain was trying to decipher the words that Dad had said. You know how when someone says something that you don't understand straightaway, but then a few seconds later your brain unscrambles the words. My brain now realised what he had said was "who is this?". I felt so upset, my heart was heavy, it was as if someone had let all the air out of a balloon! I didn't know what to do – run out into the garden, hide away, so I could be alone? I was lost, I just didn't want to go back into that room; I wanted someone to put their arm around me and tell me 'you are safe, Stewart'. I headed to the toilet, locked myself in and started to sob my heart and soul out (alone). I could still hear people talking after a while, so I went from the toilet out into the garden and just started to play 'keepy uppy' with a ball.

Then Tony and Steven (who could hear a ball bounce from ten miles away), came to the gate and gave me the look, and we went off to play by the garages, close to the milk dairy. I didn't want to go home, but Tony and Steven got called in by their mums for dinner, wash and bed, so I went home. As I walked through the backdoor, Mum said, "Where have you been, playing football out the front? You didn't say hello to your father."

I replied, "He wasn't right, something was different with him" and with this Mum said, "Stewart, come with me upstairs". She sat me down on the bed and told me that when Dad had his car crash, because he'd hit his head, the injury had affected his memory. For a short time, he was going to be like a big boy and for that she was sorry. I asked – why did he not know me, is that what happens to people in his condition, why did he not know me, but he knew Mickey and Jerry? She just looked at me, put her arm around me saying "let's go downstairs". In the front room I kept looking at Dad, but he just watched TV. We had lots of Dad's family round that night to see him, this went on till late, so we went to bed and others came and went. In the morning I came down to go to school, it was a Tuesday morning. Dad was with Mum and she said, "Len, it's Stewart; say hello, Stewart and make your father a cup of tea." There was still no acknowledgement from Dad, but I made his tea, I knew he had three sugars, very strong and it must be gold top milk. We used to have Gold Top for tea, Silver Top for drinking and Mum always said Red Top was for our Cornflakes. His cup held a pint of tea, it was a white cup with blue hoops round it.

As I handed it to him, he looked at it again and said something I didn't understand, his eyes looked at me with anger. He shoved it back at me and hot tea splashed all over my front. What have I done? I looked at Mum shocked, I could feel this really hot tea burning my chest. She grabbed the cup and my arm and said, "Come with me, Stewart" straight into the kitchen, "it's not your fault, Dad is feeling off today". Mum took my top off, gave me a clean one and she sent me off to school through the back door. I was really confused, but Mum knew best.

School was ok, I started to do well, although I still had no friends to speak of, as Tony and Steven went to another school called Westbury and Leroy left when his family moved to Brixton. Even in the playground, I was never actually asked to play anything, I would just join in. I found that the only way to be a part of the crowd was to start telling stories or lies, the bigger the story, the more time I would get with the ten-minute friends. Once I'd been grilled about the story, they'd go off and do whatever they were doing beforehand. They never wanted to carry on the conversation, or say come and play football or something else and so my opinion of myself was very low.

I started to lie; it became the normal thing to do. At home, things were not good. Mum wasn't coping with Dad at all, he was a big kid, she was looking after him all day and night and the strain was showing. He still didn't want to know me and that gave Mum problems on its own. As he was still our dad he would sometimes lash out at us, or me really, but I was used to that. As a kid, I wasn't the best kid in the world, in fact I was a little toe rag, but I often got the belt from Dad, even if I wasn't doing something wrong.

I was spending more time down with Peter and Joan, looking after Gary, Martin and Debbie as Peter and Joan would always be out with friends enjoying themselves. I think for Mum this was a very helpful way of keeping me out of the reach of Dad. I know this, as Don and Mike would often come around and take Mickey and Jerry out for the day on the weekends. Not me, but I was fine with that, as I was down at Joan and Pete's.

It was late May 1968, one Saturday morning I got up about 7am and as I came down the stairs, I could smell burnt toast. As I reached the bottom of the stairs, smoke was filling the room, and I called out to Mum "the kitchen is on fire". She came running down half-dressed, straight into the kitchen where the toaster was on fire. The fire had spread to the wallpaper at the back of the grill and above the white cooker now looked very black and sooty. Mum acted so quickly, she filled a bowl of water and put it out in seconds – fire fighters could have not done a better job! "Len," Mum cried, "what are you doing?"

"Making you breakfast," he muffled. Mum just burst into tears. "Oh, Len, I just can't cope anymore, I really can't cope, I really can't." Dad looked like a little boy who'd just been told his mother didn't love him anymore, it was so so sad at that moment. I felt for him; he'd even tried to make tea in the butter dish with butter still in it! That night, my Uncle Arthur and Dad's two brothers, Don and Mike, had a meeting in the front room. I was sent to bed with the two boys, but I sat at the top of the stairs, listening. I could hear Mum crying again. Arthur said, "It is no good, Len has to be looked after twenty-four hours a day and Gwen can no longer do that." Don said, "Len loved you and you want to put him in a home?" I wish to point out that Len was sitting with them listening to this conversation, so god knows how he was feeling. Mum said, "I need help from someone, I can't do this alone anymore. If Stewart hadn't got up this morning when he did, we all could be dead. He has also hit the kids, he's a big man with a kid mind and he is very strong, so he's always hurting Stewart most of all. He does not accept Stewart like your family, it just cannot go on anymore." Mum then said "I will not see him put in a home" then there was a knock at the door and Dad's parents came in. They went into the front room too, closing the door behind them, so I couldn't hear very much after that. I went to bed and slowly fell asleep. I awoke to the sound of the door slamming shut, so I jumped up and went to Mum's bedroom window to look out into the dark street. I just saw Don's car pulling away from the front of the house, so I crept downstairs. Mum saw my red head pop around the door and said, "Come in, Stewart." As I walked into the room, Uncle Arthur was just leaving, Mum's eyes were very red, and Dad was nowhere to be seen. "Where's Dad?" I asked. "He's gone to stay with his mother and father for a while" was the reply. My uncle patted me on the head with massive banana hands and said to me, "you be good for your mum", he got up and gave Mum a hug and then walked out the front door. "Go to bed, Stewart."

A few days passed; I was missing Dad. I went into Mum's bedroom where there was a World Cup Willie bear that Dad loved, he'd got it when he went with his brothers to watch England play football. I took the bear to school that day, so that I could take it around to him after school, as Nan and Granddad only lived half a mile away. After school, I went to see if I could see Dad. His parents lived on the first floor of the new three-storey, red brick flat fronted flats, with white windows and one entrance to a concrete stairway. I knocked on the door, my granddad opened it, and I said "Granddad". He said, "I'm not your granddad." I didn't take much notice of that comment and he added, "what do you want?" "To see Dad and give him his bear." He replied, "Well you can't see him, as we have company, I will give it to him" and with that he closed the door on me. I was a little confused, I had a lump in my throat, what did the grumpy old git mean – I'm not your granddad?

That was a really horrible moment that stayed with me for years – even to this day I can still see that encounter with him. He looked down on me with contempt, an old man and a 10-year-old boy – he must have hated me for some reason. Fucking family never made me feel welcome anyway, but I never told Mum about that evening.

Over the next few days we were in a state of limbo around the house. Mum was always crying herself to sleep at night, I could hear her in bed. I wanted to go in and see her, but she'd always send me back to my bedroom. Things were different now it was not going to change or get any better in the foreseeable future. We had no income and Mum was going to get a job. No benefits then, just get on with it, the order of the day!

I was not happy at school anymore. I didn't want to go, so I started to bunk off every other day and play over at the building sites. Men onsite would pay me to go and get tea and be a general 'gofer'. This was a new building site and I knew some of the lads from the last site. Then one day, a bricklayer fell off the scaffolding and the Safety Officer told me that I wasn't allowed on site anymore. So, because of the dangers onsite, I lost my place to go in the daytime. I needed money to play out with other kids that bunked off school, they would buy a red rover bus ticket, which would let you go anywhere in London for the day. No one would think it was strange, to see young boys or girls of 10 years old, either on a bus traveling alone or in a small group. I couldn't just come out and ask for the money, that might be a giveaway, so I started to take money from Mum's bag. Just a few pennies to start with, then gradually I started to take more – it was like a drug that I needed. Mum was beginning to notice, and she pulled me to one side and told me off. It was then that it all came out about me bunking off school, so I was grounded for two weeks. I would come home from school and have to go straight to my bedroom, only coming down for tea, plus she took me to school every day to make sure that I got there. I was good for a few weeks after the grounding had finished, but as with most kids (that I knew anyway), as the weeks passed by, I slipped back into taking money. My mum even started to take her bag to bed with her, but I would creep into her bedroom in the early morning and take money while she slept. It became too much for Mum; she reached breaking point after putting her bag underneath her pillow and I still managed to slide my hand under her head, remove the bag, take the money and put the bag back without waking her up. I was taken to see the doctor, who gave my mum the name of a psychiatrist and it was decided that to give Mum a rest, I should go and stay with Uncle Arthur and Nan for a few weeks at their place, which was a prefab in Barking. My first day at Nan's place was very different from home . . . to describe my Nan: she was an old country girl at heart, never really got used to town life, she was about sixty, used a walking stick, wore glasses and had brushed back grey hair in a bun. I would say this could describe 90% of most grandmothers around the country at that time – everyone looked the same after they passed their forties. As for my uncle, he was big, had been an Officer in the Guards, served in the Korean war, was about six foot six and had hands like two shovels. He was a very quiet man, who filled the room with his size, personality and kind soul. Finally, there was Sue the dog, an old English Sheep dog. Sue and I had an understanding – she could only bite me if I was alone with her, then I could fight back. I never won but she would bite me on the arm or leg. She never broke my skin; it was just a game and nicking her bones was not a good idea!

It was the last half term before the six-week holiday. I knew at Nan's place it was going to be hard work, cutting the grass, having a bath every day. Having your nan always looking behind your ears to see if they're clean and your teeth and between your toes – I was very clean! During the next few weeks, two of my girl cousins would often come to see Nan too; Linda was the oldest, she was about ten years older than me, and Elaine who was the same age as me. To describe Linda, she was a redhead and was very nice in every way, she was like the old saying 'sugar and spice and all things nice', that describes her best, I had a lot of time for Linda. We got on very well, she was the closest to being a sister you could ever get and we had a lot of fun. As for Elaine, she was the same height as me with long blonde hair and what she thought was a big nose. She was totally different to Linda, we would fight verbally a lot, she was always right, never wrong, you know, a typical know-it-all.

It was a weekend and Elaine had come to visit Nan. As she walked into the prefab, she clapped eyes on me and gave me a very funny look. She walked over, gave Nan a kiss on the cheek and sat down next to me. I felt very unsure as she said, "Coming out in the garden to play?" I said, "ok" and as we went out, I heard Nan say, 'no fighting'. "Stewart, let's go around the back and play." "Why?" I asked. "Because I want you to do something for me." I felt that whatever it was I would pay for it. As we stopped by an old oak tree in the garden she said, "Stewart, if I give you some money, could you do something for me?"

"Like what?"

"Well, remember the last time I saw you, you told me that people pay money to have their nose broken and it makes the nose smaller?"

"Oh yes I remember."

"Well if I give you three pennies could you do it to me?"

I was never going to turn down money, so I agreed. Once she gave me the money, I told Elaine to lie down on the floor under the tree, then I picked up my brother Jerry's metal toy shovel and hit her right on the nose. She let out such a scream I was sure that the windows would shatter and my eardrums pop. Uncle Arthur had just walked in from work; he came dashing round the side of the house and saw me standing over Elaine's body – she was out cold.

"What's been going on?" he demanded, but before I could say a word, I was told to get in the house, and I was not going to argue with him. Nan standing by the back door asked, "What have you been up to? Get inside." I could hear them talking outside. In the kitchen, Elaine had come around and was now leaning over the sink dripping blood into the running water.

"Stewart, come out here, do you know that you've broken her nose?"

"She wanted me to."

Nan hit me on the bum with her walking stick; it didn't hurt but I jumped up and down to make it look good! I got away with it, Elaine never said a word and she knew I'd get it from Nan. I had the money, so she could not say anything, or she would get it too. Elaine stayed that night, in the same bed as me but we did not talk very much. In the morning I was up first. Arthur would make himself tea with egg and bacon on toast; if I was in the kitchen when he was making it, I would always get some. When Elaine came into the kitchen, I started laughing at her two very black eyes and fat nose – Henry Cooper could not have done a better job. I could see that Uncle Arthur was trying not to laugh. The look Elaine gave me said she wanted to kill me but instead she said, "You little rat, you told me that my nose would get shorter if I broke it." That was it, Arthur exploded with laughter, he just went off. Elaine stamped her foot on the ground, turned around and called out to Nan, even the dog, Sue, was barking at her as Nan came into the kitchen; we tried to stop laughing but we couldn't. Sue the dog ran out into the garden. "Coward, Arthur," she said. "You should know better." He got up and had to leave the room for a minute in order to stop laughing. I got told off, and when he came back to the kitchen Arthur had his front teeth clamped down on his bottom lip and as we sat around the table no-one could look at Elaine.

Nan said, "I think you had better go out and play when Elaine's 'Mum May' and 'Dad Chick' come to pick her up." I kept out of the way until everyone had gone.

Nan had received a letter to say that she could have her hip operation which would mean that she did not need her walking stick anymore; it also meant that she would not be hitting me round the backside any more either with it, so that was good news, plus they had just been told that they were going to get a new ground floor flat on the Barking Estate, the very one I had been working on.

The day came when I went back home, things went back to normal, I went back to school and Mum seemed to be coping with most things apart from me not behaving. I had my first appointment with the psychiatrist and I didn't know what a straitjacket keeper was. Mum took me to the reception area for about ten minutes and I was getting more nervous by the minute. Then a little man came into the room and asked Mum to see him alone and left me in reception for a moment. For the next five minutes, I was straining my ears off trying to hear what was being said about me, until Mum came out of the room saying, "Stewart you can go in now, I will be out here." "Why am I going in alone?" I asked. "It's ok," the doctor said, "your mum knows everything I'm going to say to you." As I walked in, it had a feeling of doom about it, 'your last supper' sort of thing, and the walls were covered with lots of pictures of animals. The desk was in the centre of the room and in the corner was a small table with chairs around it and what looked like lots of games and books stacked on it. I was told to sit down over by the books then he asked, "Do you like your school?"

"Yes," I replied, and he wrote in his notebook.

"What do you think your position is at home?"

"I am the big boy of the house – I must help my mum."

"Why do you bunk off school?"

"Because I no longer like school, the teachers don't like me whatsoever and I can't keep up with the rest of the class."

"Would you like to change schools?"

"Why do you ask?"

"Maybe we could find you a school that would help with your progress; when you've caught up with everyone in class, you'll feel better about yourself."

I didn't even get the chance to reply, as he stood up and said, "Could you call your mum in" and then Mum came into the room with a questioning look on her face.

The doctor then asked me to wait outside and I replied, "No, if you're going to talk about me, I want to hear it."

The doctor looked very shocked at what I'd said; he looked at Mum, his mouth dropped open – I think it must have been the first time he'd been lost for words.

"Go outside, Stewart." Mum looked at me with eyes that zeroed in on me like a bullet from a gun, I understood that look, so I left the room! After about two minutes, she came out with a very strange look on her face and said, "Come on, let's go." As we walked out the heavens opened up and the rain just poured down as we ran to the bus stop. We just got there as a bus pulled up and we sat upstairs.

"Stewart, would you like to go to a new school that would help you?"

"Yes, but I don't know any schools around here that are any good." Well Abbey School was a bit better, or so I was told. "But Mum, I'll go to a new school next year anyway, I am going to be 11."

"This school is one that you will have to live at."

"What?! No way, Mum."

"Look, it would be for your own good."

What a bombshell to drop and she asked me to think about it. I had just started to get my head around that small problem when she said, "I have something to tell you about your dad, you know Uncle Red (short for Fred), he is your father, and Len is your brothers' father."

I was so lost for words I just sat there, I didn't know what to say or do, cry or scream, I just couldn't take it in. She was saying that the uncle who always let me down, never came to see me when he said he would and just left me out to dry was my father! It all fell into place and a feeling of hatred came over me. I never said any more to Mum on the subject because Nan was going in for her hip operation the very next day and Uncle Arthur was moving to a new flat over the weekend. I gave Arthur a hand, as did most of the family, in order to get the new flat ready for Nan when she came out of hospital. On the Monday, we all went to see Nan in King George's Hospital. She was doing well after the operation, it was good to see her happy and looking forward to coming home to her new flat; but when we got home that night Mum suddenly said she must ring the hospital. "Something is wrong," she said, "look after your brothers a minute" and she ran out the door. I looked up the road and I could see she'd gone to the payphone at the end of the road. About twenty minutes later, Mum came back and said that she had to go and get Arthur and then get back to the hospital as soon as possible, then she shot out the door, down to Peter and Joan to see if we could stay with them for the night (which we did). In the morning, when we got home Mum and Arthur were there holding each other while Mum sobbed. "What's up?" I asked. "Your nan died last night" was the reply, then Arthur started to cry too. This was too much for me, I couldn't handle any more; I just wanted to hide away but Mum was in no fit state, so I would help with my brothers and around the house – I had to be the strong one. After a few days, Nan was laid to rest at Barking Cemetery and I started to reflect on the situation around my life, that my dad was not my dad and my uncle was my dad. The penny started to drop about all the times my brothers would spend with Len's family and I was always pushed aside, left out. At a young age, to know you were not wanted at all felt hard.

It was becoming more apparent that Mum could no longer cope with us, all the stress of what had happened over this past year was just too much, she had a kidney problem the needed hospital attention every few months, plus high blood pressure.

Mum had started to feel a little bit better after a few weeks, she was getting on with life like she always did, it was Saturday morning and it was raining hard outside. I heard Mum call out to me, so I went to her room. She was lying on the bed, holding her tummy and there was blood on the bed. "Get someone, Stewart, get help quickly." so in a panic I ran across the road to Tony's house – his mother Elaine was a good friend to Mum. It was 7am so nobody was up, I kept banging on the door for probably seconds, which felt like hours to me. The door was burst open by John, the boyfriend. "Stewart," he growled, "Tony is still in bed." He was standing in front of me half asleep in his pants. "No, no, it's my mum, she's in bed and she is bleeding and crying."

"Hold on," he said, grabbed the first thing to hand and started to run down the road to our house. He did look a sight wearing Elaine's yellow dressing gown and bare feet! As he ran across the road, he stepped right into a pile of dog crap, he slid on one leg, crashing into our front gate! John just rubbed his foot on the grass in our front garden to clean it off the best he could and went into the house. At the bottom of the stairs, he called up to Mum that he was coming up and as he walked into the bedroom and saw all the blood, he said to me, "Stay with your mum, I'm going to call for an ambulance." Mum just lay in bed crying in pain, Elaine came over to sit with her and John had washed his smelling foot and put jeans on, by the time an ambulance arrived and took Mum off to hospital. Elaine went with her and John stayed with us until Arthur turned up to see what was going on. After four or five hours, Mum came home in a taxi with Elaine. She looked very pale and weak and went straight to bed (which had been cleaned and changed by John). Elaine explained to Uncle Arthur that it was a small haemorrhage and that she would be alright, she just needed rest. Over the next few days, John would pop in to see if we were all ok and speak to Mum. He was a good man, everyone liked him. He ran his own demolition company and they were pulling down four streets to make way for a new low-rise three-storey block of flats in Barking. Something, however, must have happened between Elaine and him because he left. I still saw him working on the site, though. I would go and see him and on

43

weekends I would help burn the rubbish. It was such a Saturday morning and I was helping John as usual, he was up on a party wall, about thirty feet high. He called out for me to fetch the flask of coffee from his truck, as he'd be down in a minute, but as he started to walk across the top of the wall, the bottom gave way and the wall began to fall over like a felled tree! In a split second, John ran down the wall, it looked funny to me, I thought he was messing about, until he hit the ground with timber and slates crashing down until you couldn't see him. There was a giant dust ball everywhere. I shouted "John!" He called out, "Stay where you are, it's not safe, I'm alright" – and he walked out of the dust and smoke with two panda like eyes, looking like he'd been down the mines.

We sat down together on two barrels, and he said, "God was on my side today." It was then I spotted the cuts on his back so I said, "We'd better go home to my house." Mum could patch him up, as she'd got good at that over the years, but I didn't tell him she loved using TCP to clean! Or was it only on me, 'mmmm'? He slowly eased himself into the truck and drove off, stopping outside my house while I ran in telling Mum. She came out and called John in, she cleaned him up and told him he needed to go to the hospital to get some of the cuts stitched up. He said, "Ok, only if you come with me to hold my hand?" After that day, we saw a lot more of John, he was a good friend to my brothers and I – it was also good to see Mum smiling again.

This day would be my first encounter with sex. My brothers and I would go swimming on Friday evenings, usually we would go for hours, but today I forgot my trunks, so I came home to get them. As I walked in the back door, I noticed clothes on the floor in the front room and I could hear talking, so I started to go upstairs – being a good average ten-year-old, I needed to see what was going on! I crept to the top of the stairs, slowly looked round the bedroom door, and I was gob-smacked – there was John lying on top of Mum going up and down and she was moaning, well not moaning but saying some things like 'not too hard, John'! I sat watching for a few moments, then thought I better leave as quietly as I could.

Over the next few weeks things were good at home, I was still seeing the psychiatrist, but today's trip to see him was different. He told me it had been decided I should go to boarding school. "What do you mean?" I asked.

"It means that you'll go away to school for a short time."

"How long am I going for?"

"As long as it takes to help you, your Mum has a man around the house now to help out and you don't need to worry about her anymore."

"Why me? What have I done wrong?"

He didn't look at me and spoke to Mum instead. "It's for the best and it will help you both out in the long run."

Then we got up and left. I never said a word to anyone for a few days. I had two weeks to get myself together, before I was off to the new school in Rotherwick, Hampshire. The weekend before I was due to leave, we bought my new school uniform and new clothes. Mum took me to a place in London, where they had loads of uniforms hanging on the wall, I tried on everything, four white shirts, four black trousers, two pairs of black leather lace up shoes, socks, loads of pants and two school ties (navy blue with green stripes and a green school badge with a crest on it). Mum had to write a number in everything, 38 was the number. John moved in with Mum, she was happy, my brothers were being good, and Mick was starting school this new term as well. My friends knew I was off to school soon and Steven said to me, "I've got something for you, do you want to come to my house – Mum and Dad are out?" His sister was in the front room wearing a dress, she was 13 years old, tall with blonde hair. "My sister Tracey said, if you like, she will show you her fanny if you let her see yours."

"What?!" First of all, I've never even seen a naked girl and I didn't think that way. So, I said ok (as you do to look big, in front of your mate), she stood up and just lifted her dress and pulled down her knickers; all I saw was this hedgehog and I started laughing. She pulled up her knickers and said, "Let me see yours." I just pulled down my shorts as I had no pants on, she looked at this little worm and just walked away. Nothing was said ever – what a non-event.

We all then went off to the Saturday morning pictures in Barking, 11am – 1pm. We all used to go once every two weeks, but some people would go every week. It was a good morning, just kids with their entry fee and we got a small drink and a mixed bag of sweets. The things we saw each time were, Flash Gordon, Laurel and Hardy, and The Lone Ranger – Oh yes and Daffy Duck or Bugs Bunny– and it was always packed. You would get ushers walking up and down the aisle with torches, making sure kids weren't up to no good. Mums and dads would be outside smoking in the lobby, waiting for the kids to come out, but most of us would walk home for miles. This was my last weekend at home, before I started the new school and said goodbye to my friends. Tony said, "Let's take one of the milk floats for a drive." It was Sunday evening; the milk floats were always out the front, with power cables going from the floats over the metal green fence, to the charging points in the Dairy, allowing the deliveries in at night. Steven said, "Tony you're not driving, I am!" Steve sat in the driver's seat, me and Tony jumped on the flat back and we were off, 10 miles an hour, flying up the road! Coming down the other side of the road, believe it or not was a bloody panda car, bloody police.

Steven stopped dead and both of us fell forward and off the side. Before we hit the ground, we were on our toes and over the 6′ garden fence, down the alley and around the back into my garden. We never got caught! I said, "Lads, it's been a blast, see you in a few weeks." I gave them my football, as Mickey and Jerry never played football. My brothers and I were a little distant, because they used to spend a lot of time with their dad's family. Now Dad had gone, the family just never made contact anymore – nice people. It didn't matter much for me, but Jerry and Mick didn't understand. One minute, every other day and on weekends they were with Dad's family and then they were just cut off. Maybe it was for the best, but it was upsetting for them. I knew Mum would make it right, as she always did. Mum had that way about her, Mickey always needed more attention than Jerry – Mickey was a Mummy's boy to be honest!

CHAPTER THREE

Boarding School

THE BIG DAY WAS HERE. Monday morning, I put my new school uniform on – it felt strange; I said goodbye to Mickey and Jerry, but they didn't understand what was going on, they thought I was going on holiday. We walked to the bus stop, me wearing my new uniform, carrying a little brown suitcase with a small cardboard name tag. Number 87 arrived, we jumped on it to get to Barking Station, then the underground train to Waterloo. Very apt for how I was feeling; the letter we had received said to be at Gate 6 by 10.15am and for once London Underground was running like clockwork and it got me there right on time. I'd never seen Waterloo Station before, it was massive to me, I'd never seen such a mega structure before. There were steel green columns rising up from the ground like towering trees, supporting smoky, dusty glass and a steel roof full of pigeons. The people were in a rush and there were smells of diesel fumes and people smoking. People were waiting around for trains, dodging each other, heading off to wherever, with sounds of whistles blowing when trains were leaving. Speakers announcing trains, but I just couldn't understand what they were saying, it was too muffled. We found Gate 6, there were 80 or so other boys with the same school uniform on as me. I knew I was no longer dreaming; a sinking feeling came over me (this is real). As we reached the crowd of boys and their parents, a man with a clipboard came over to us

THE LIFE OF A SCREWBALL

and asked, "Is this Stewart?" "Yes," Mum replied. "My name is Mr Jenkins, I'm one of the teachers, don't worry, Mrs Byrne, we'll take good care of him. We'll be leaving in about ten minutes." Mr Jenkins was about 5'8" and a very powerful looking man. He had a kind, but beaten up face (looked like it had been put through a blending machine), his voice was gruff – you could tell he was Welsh. He made me feel a little better. The station loudspeakers said something, and we all started to move down towards the platform. I started to feel a bit sick as we walked along, with a feeling inside of dread. I'd never been on an Intercity – 8 carriage – British Rail train before. It was a kind of blue green on the bottom half and had a white stripe from the start of the windows to the top and then green blue again. There were loads of doors with pull down windows, bench seats from one door across the train to the other door. It was like a tube, no access to the next carriage, not even a toilet (Cattle Class). The heavy doors had brass handles, that you had to twist to get open and no safety locks inside. I took my case from Mum and got on into the train, putting my case on the floor. A teacher then put them up on the shelves above the seats, as we were too short to do that.

Twenty children and a teacher in one section (a bit cramped) – I was lucky, I got the window seat. Saying goodbye to Mum, this was the very first time I'd ever had to say goodbye. I put my arms around her and squeezed her as hard as I could, as she held me close; I wanted to cry, I felt I was losing her forever. Then a guard shouted 'all aboard', blew his whistle and she said, "Come on, Stewart, be good for me" so I let go of her and stepped onto the train. All that I could hear were doors slamming; click bang, click bang, click bang, click bang, as the guard wearing a black uniform with silver buttons and a black cap with the British Rail cap badge walked along the platform, closing the open doors. I knew my mother was being brave – her eyes gave it away, her eyes were red and full of tears. As I sat in my seat, I looked at her and she gave me a smile, kissed her hand and put it to her lips to blow it to me, then the train shunted forwards and we started to move off. With that, my heart started to turn to stone, I watched and waved to Mum as we slowly moved out of the long-curved platform and she disappeared behind baggage trolleys as we picked up speed.

With a sinking feeling in my heart, I sat looking out of the window; clickerty clack, clickerty clack, as the train crossed over other rails. One of the boys sitting next to me said, "Hello, my name is Randy Goldman, are you a new boy too?"

"Yes," I replied.

"What's your name?"

"Stewart."

Randy was about 12 years old with very short black hair, round thick bottle lens glasses, with a nose that took all the free air in that it could get. He had a smile that made friends instantly. I remember at the time he was a very funny lad, but he had fingernails that any woman would be proud of – they must have been half an inch long but a bit grubby! We talked all the way to Hook Station, mostly about nothing, but wondering what we were in for. This took just over an hour or so, to pull into Hook station. Hook station was very, very sparse, with a large hanging clock and flower baskets under the canopy. We got straight off and went through an open steel gate, onto five coaches that were waiting for everyone in the car park. It would take about half an hour to get from the station to the front gates and as we were weaving through the country lanes, the number of houses I saw became fewer and the air was full of countryside smells. At 2pm, we arrived at an old 8′ tall, proud looking brick and sandstone structure, that used to hold large metal gates, to a driveway fit for a royal family! TYLNEY HALL was carved into the stone section on one of the pillars. "We're here," said one of the teachers, to those sitting at the front. As we drove down the long drive, that had seen better days, with a few big potholes that were filled with sand, the sun was flickering through the tall redwood trees, that were towering and stretching out in front of us. They were about twenty feet apart and must have been 100 feet high × 10 feet wide – all along the long driveway, guiding you up to the school forecourt. Whoever owned this place in the past, must have walked down this drive – they must have felt like they had everything!

As the building came into view and we drove out from the drive onto the forecourt, I just remember it was breathtaking. I thought, my God, it's a palace! The building itself stood proud, boasting of wealth and power from past days. The mansion was a u-shape, four storeys high, red brick with a sandstone frontage window surrounds and black metal framed Georgian windows. In the centre were huge arch-shaped, dark oak front doors with two heavy black round door knockers and black studs. The roof had chimneys towering high, with lightning conductors pointing straight up towards the heavens. We all then got off the coach, picking up our luggage from the rear, and standing in front of the main doors were about 10 staff. As I looked around, I stood in the centre of a monstrous building. It made you take a deep breath and you could feel the history of this place – it was overwhelming! Three senior boys who had lists in their hands, started calling out names. "If you hear your name, come and stand behind us."

Once everyone's name had been called and they had stood behind the right Senior, all seemed to be accounted for and we were told to follow them. One line of what looked like older boys went back down the drive, then through another gate entrance to the lower blocks behind the main school building. They were classed as seniors, they were over 14, we were junior, and we were taken to a side door in the main building, then up eight flights. These were solid white painted and deep blue carpeted stair treads, each half landing had a newel post, with a white cannon ball side cap and a handrail of varnished oak. On the way up, we passed two other landings, one was to the classrooms and the other was to the sick bay and staff accommodation. The stairwell had a glass skylight that allowed the sun to just beam in. At the top, we walked from carpet, onto a deep red vinyl flooring, leading to a long corridor that stretched out in front of us. There were white doors with names of birds on each side of the corridor; these were the dormitories.

A scruffy, bearded middle-aged man, with a plump body, came out of a side room to greet us with yet another clipboard; "My name is Mr Ogden, I look after you at night and on weekends. When I call out your name and dorm, you can go and find a bed, see your dorm leader and he will tell you what to do." My dormitory was called Falcon, all the bedrooms had names of birds of prey, then walking into the dorm a boy called Gary Shavell stopped me and said, "I'm your dormitory leader, what is your name?"

"Stewart."

"Your bed is the one at the far end, under the window."

The dorm was about twenty metres long, by ten metres wide, with ten beds, five on each side, in a dead straight line and each bed had a small wooden locker next to it. The walls were painted cream and the floor was red linoleum and there was a speaker on the wall playing classical music. When all the boys were in the Dorm, Gary closed the door and said, "I'll fill you in on the rules. We get up at 6.30am Monday to Friday and on Saturday and Sunday you get a lie in until 7.30am. Your school clothes go to the linen room, which is back down the corridor towards the door that you came in. You change your uniform twice a week and make sure that your shoes are always clean and polished ready for inspection. Breakfast is at 7.30am, dinner is at 12, tea is at 4pm and supper is at 7pm. Everyone is to be up in the dorm by 8pm and lights are out at 9pm. We have dormitory inspections every morning, your beds must be made, and floors swept. Your bedding gets changed twice a week and that's all I can tell you at this point."

It was late afternoon; I had made my bed for the very first time – we were shown once how to make it. Two white crisp sheets, one blanket and an over cover blanket (blue or yellow). One pillow with a white case, the bottom sheet had to be tight and the top sheet with hospital corners. The bed should look like a box, top flat and folded in the right places. I put my things away then we all got called for supper by the dormitory leader.

We all filed down to the ground level and out to the main forecourt outside. They informed us as we walked out what the three lines down the forecourt were. Line one, Stuart House line; York House, Line two; and Tudor House Line three. I was Stuart house; I think because I had a green crested blazer badge. One of the seniors was the House Captain, and he was walking up and down the line counting us. He called out, "Sir, all present and correct for numbers." This was repeated to the member of staff outside the front of the building. The lines all faced the front of the main doors, the staff entrance. Mr Scott was a member of staff, he was a short, rotund man, with red fuzzy hair – it looked like a mushroom on his head!

One house at a time filed off to the dining room, which was an L shaped room, with thirty tables set out. Each table was set with eight places, three each side and one at each end, and every table had a table leader, who would sit at the head of the table. Fifth year boys only, they were fully responsible for the table and us, they were all the head boys. We were told to just find a table today, because everything would be sorted out on Tuesday.

Supper, we had bacon, beans and bread with jam – plus a white mug of tea that would clean out a blocked drain! After supper had finished, we had to clear the tables and we were told to stack our plates, cups and cutlery at the end table. The table leaders would show us what to do in the future and this was the only time they would do so – "take note" we were told.

Gavin was the name of our table leader. He stood at the end of the table and one of the kitchen staff stood at the entrance to the dining room with a trolley. Mr Ogden, who was standing in the centre of the dining room, said "cutlery" and all the table leaders picked up the cutlery and carried it to the trolley, placing it on top. They then went back to the table until "plates" were called, and so on, until all the items were cleared from the table and we were dismissed, a table at a time. On weekdays, you had to go back to the dorms after supper because of school in the morning, but weekends you could go out or do something for a few hours before going back upstairs.

This was my first night away from home. I wondered what Mum was thinking and were my brothers ok. I sat on my bed putting my things away, feeling a bit homesick and sorry for myself. Anyone that has felt homesick will tell you, it's a cross between being dumped by your best friends and being abandoned. Some of the new boys, like me, were also sitting around not saying very much and looking lost. It was about 9pm – "lights out" the staff called down the corridor, and lads filed out of the TV Room after watching TV.

"So, everyone must get back to their dorms and into bed." We had two men who looked after us at night, Mr Ogden and Mr Scott; they had rooms on our floor. Mr Ogden was a fat man with a big smiling face, he made you feel like he was your friend and Mr Scott was a young man, full of life, always having a joke with everyone. His nickname was Fuzzy because of his hair. As they came into the rooms and turned off the lights, they said, "All you new boys, the first night is always tough, but it does get better with time, goodnight." After the lights went out, music started coming out of the speakers on the wall, then a voice came over the air, it was one of the boys. He was going to read a bedtime story from a book, he read for about fifteen minutes then everything went quiet. This was done every night, Monday till Friday. As the moon flooded through my open window, casting a shadow on the floor and my bed, I was thinking I wanted to go home. I wanted to cry, I felt alone, unwanted, got rid of, out of the way, out of sight out of mind. I could hear one of the other boys sniffing, the telltale sign of crying into pillows, not wanting to be ridiculed. Over in the far corner it was very quiet. Randy got up and went to the toilet, a bare foot sound on vinyl flooring, so I followed him to see if he was ok. As we both opened the dorm door and went out into the corridor, Mr Ogden and Mr Scott were there talking to other boys that were upset. This went on for the next few nights, until everyone settled in. I spoke to Randy in the corridor and he felt just like me. I think that helped both of us to know that most kids felt the same when they arrived at first. We both went back to our beds, slowly the other boys started to drift off to sleep. The night became very still and all I could hear through the open window was the wind blowing through the trees; I drifted off to sleep. Then suddenly the door burst open, in came Mr Scott – "come on, get up" as he went around pulling off everyone's bed covers saying, "hands off cocks and on socks". That must be one of the best quotes I have ever read on a toilet wall! This was the first morning for me, pick up your towel and toothbrush, then head off to the washrooms and showers. The bathroom was about 30′ square with white floor tiles, grey painted walls and three rows of small sinks back to back. I would say approximately 30 sinks and a shower block of 10 shower heads in a row and 5 baths. The soap was an odourless small white bar. You needed to get yourself ready, make your bed and you should have cleaned your shoes the night before. We all filed downstairs to breakfast; scrambled egg and bread with yes, the old strong tea. After breakfast we all went back upstairs for the dorm inspection and uniform inspection.

THE FIRST DAY AT SCHOOL

After the dorm inspections, we were all sent out to the forecourt, the same one that we'd arrived at by coach the previous day. We all stood around talking to each other, Randy, me and a John Coal who was also in our dorm. The teachers came out of the main doors at the front of the building, then the whistle blew three short blasts and in a regimental bellowing voice Mr Jenkins shouted, "stand still". He stood looking around after his orders and we were told to stand dead still until we heard the second whistle – it seemed an age! On the second blast we should form our House lines, except today as we just formed three lines until we found out which House we were going to be in. Three teachers were holding badges in their hands. Mr Bingham said, "When your name is called out, go to Mrs Baker, for Stuart House; Mr Jenkins for York House; and Mr Barker for Tudor House. We were all split up, Randy was York, John was Tudor, and I was Stuart House. From now on, every time the whistle blew, we would form three lines on the forecourt – facing the teachers, at the front of the building. Our House Captain was a fifth-year boy called Graham Sharp; he was about five foot ten with blond hair and a face that looked like the surface of the moon. He shouted a lot! The line had to be dead straight and an arms-length from the person in front of you or dress off. This would happen five times a day, every day – for the end of every break, tea, dinner and assembly. We had assembly in the main hall; it was big, like walking into a church, with dark wood panelled walls, ceiling 10 metres high and a staff stage. Three lines of chairs were set out in House order, Stuart were in the centre row. At the front of the Hall was a stage for the staff to look down on us, with a piano. The Headmaster Mr Kirby entered the room and someone at the back shouted "attention", and we all stood up and waited for him to take his place on the stage before we sat down again. I was overwhelmed with all the pomp and fuss. We were then told all the rules and regulations, the do's and don'ts. Then at the end of the briefing the Headmaster said, "we have a new boy called Stewart, he is the youngest boy to ever come to this school, he is only ten, so keep an eye out for him. He's the ginger one over there in Stuart House." I could have died as everyone looked at me!

After assembly we all filed out to the forecourt to play tip and run cricket, or football or maybe beat up a new boy (I think that was one of the sports). We just hung around, did whatever we wanted to. As we walked out, the sun was shining, and the air smelt clean. Some of the boys started to play cricket in the centre of the forecourt, three white lines chalked on the wall as the wicket; I would say about 80% of the boys played. Randy and I had started to walk across the forecourt, when one of the older boys came over to us and he had that bully look about him! "You two come over here." He was about 15 feet from us; I didn't move. Randy said, "Come on" and I replied, "No, wait for him to come here."

He came closer. "Did you hear me, new farts?"

"What's a new fart?" I said and I started to grin like a cat.

"What's a new fart? It's all new boys for the first term," he said.

"Oh, ok," I replied. "You listen to me, you little ginger twerp, you do what I say, or I will beat the living daylights out of you."

He was bigger, older and even better looking than me, so I said, "Ok, what do you want us to do?"

"Anything I want you to do – ok."

Randy looked at me; Nick was the boy's name and he was full of his own importance. "I'm the best fighter in the juniors," he bragged.

"So what?" I said, which turned out to be the wrong thing to have said.

He came over and pushed me up against the wall. "You listen to me, you little rat, if you don't want a good kicking, keep your gob shut, got it?"

I didn't say a word, I just looked him right in the eyes. I think he was just about to try and flatten my nose when Mr Campbell came over. "Everything ok, boys?"

I said "yes" and Nick walked away, but I knew by the way he was look-ing back at me, that we were going to meet again very soon – he kept looking at me across the forecourt with those 'I am going to kick your teeth in' eyes. The whistle blew, we all lined up to listen to our names and join our class teacher for this year. I got Mr Jenkins, the Welshman, about five foot eight, stocky with dark hair, about 60 years old and used to play for the British Lions (Oh yes, he had all the hallmarks, a flat nose and cauliflower ears).

"Come with me, boys, to your classroom, up on the first floor."

We walked down the long oak floor corridor, with white panelling halfway up the wall, finished off in magnolia painted walls. The ceiling was high, all doors were solid and heavy looking with panels with round brass doorknobs. Our classrooms were at the end of the corridor.

"This is your form classroom for this year, come in, find a desk, sit down and be quiet."

The views from the classroom were stunning: we looked down a green vista, lines of trees like a runway, just a shame the furniture was not up to the same standard as the building (just school desks and chairs, as every other school up and down the country). After a long day, figuring out the week's timetable, the teacher's names, the rules etc, it was finally time for tea, but before that, the table leaders had to pick the boys they wanted on their table for the year. I was put on David Brady's, he was a big blond-haired lad with a flat face, a pigeon chest and a bit of a big head, to say the least. Oh yes, he had the mouth to go with it, but all in all – he was good to me. Also, on our table was Nick the Neanderthal; I had forgotten about him. He sat right opposite me, he was at least two years older than me – plus much bigger. He kicked me under the table, so I kicked him back; he jumped. "You bastard, you wait till you get outside." I wasn't worried, I knew I would get into a fight sooner or later. We all went up to our dorms after tea and changed into our old clothes. We had free time to play football, or go in the woods and grounds. Nick came to our dorm and said, "I will see you round at the old tennis courts in ten minutes, got it?" As I arrived at the courts, I could see a gang of about twenty boys all waiting to see the fight, Randy and John were with me and I was now beginning to feel a bit sick. I was within ten feet of him, when he came at me, grabbed me around the waist like a rugby tackle and shoved me up against the wall. I felt pain in the back of my head, as it impacted on the wall, then he let go and punched me on the lower part of the chin. I knew then that this kid's punches could not hurt me, so I grabbed him round the neck, pulling him to the ground, hitting him in the stomach, head, leg and in his balls! It took the wind out of him, it was a lucky punch; he was having trouble getting his breath, so I got off him and just walked away. All his friends just stood and looked at him, as I went off with the two boys. In retrospect, I should have lost that fight because everyone then wanted to fight me, every other day someone seemed to want to punch my head in. Some fights I won, others I drew, but I didn't ever lose a fight outright because, to beat me, you would have to kill me – I would just keep on coming whatever you did to me! After a few weeks, nobody wanted to fight me anymore and I would like to point out that we're only talking about Juniors.

Within a few months, I'd got into the everyday running of things, I just fitted in like everyone else. As I got accepted, more and more doors opened and I started to make friends; you got to play 'war' in the woods with about twenty other boys, plus cricket at play time.

I was still the youngest in the school, most of the boys were teenagers and I didn't understand what the moaning sounds were, coming from some of the beds at night! Until one of the boys (Terry) said that he had had four wanks that night and then some others started to say that they had had five or six. I could hear this conversation going on, so I asked, "what is a wank?" just as Mr Ogden walked into the dorm. "Something that makes you go blind if you have too many," he said. All the boys looked at me. "Lights out, boys," he added as he left the room.

After he'd gone everyone started to laugh and a pillow came out of the darkness and hit me smack in the face. The next morning being Saturday, I was going to find out what the big joke was, but everyone I asked said, "if you don't know, you're a wanker". I was getting nowhere, so I went to sick bay where the nurse Mrs Jenkins was. I knew it was something rude.

"Hello what is up with you today, Stewart?" she asked. "I can't see any blood or black eyes."

"Miss, can I ask you something? I think it's rude."

"What is it, spit it out."

"What is a wank?"

Shocked, she said, "Get out, you little disgusting boy, I will speak to the Head about you on Monday."

My biggest problem now was going to be when she tells her old man. He was going to kick my backside into orbit. Mr Jenkins had a way of sorting you out, he would grab you by the hair and shake your head up and down, side to side, saying "by jove, my lad, don't you mess with me"! All day, I kept away from the area he lived, then about tea time, when we were heading back to the forecourt from the woods, I'd totally forgotten what had happened in the morning, when I heard "Mr Byrne, my lad, come here". I froze on the spot. "Oh crap," John said, "what have you done?"

"You wouldn't believe me if I told you, but I think I am in for a shake, rattle and smack," I replied, and I walked slowly towards Mr Jenkins.

"Come on, man, move it."

I tried to brace myself for the inevitable.

"Come with me." And we went upstairs to sick bay. Mrs Jenkins was sitting in the surgery.

"Now then, boy, what did you say to Mrs Jenkins?" he asked, so as I told him, I felt my heart start to pump faster and my face was getting red and overheating. I was waiting for the big bang, then all of a sudden Mr Jenkins began to chuckle. "I am telling you, my boy, if anyone other than you had said that, I'd have given them a piece of my mind. Go outside a minute, boy, I need to talk to the nurse."

I sat outside for a few minutes, I could hear some mumbling and laughing, then the door opened.

"Come in, son." Mrs Jenkins left the room. "Now then, boy, I am going to give you the answer to your question," he said. "What your friends call wanking is another word for masturbating, you know what your penis is? Well some mornings you get up and you find that it is stiff and hard, this is called an erection. What some of the boys (or most of them judging by the smiles on their faces) do in the morning, is play with themselves, so that they get an erection and bring themselves to orgasm. That's the best I can say to describe it to you, and you are still too young to understand. Do you understand?"

I nodded yes, but I had no clue really, he was right.

Then: "Off with you, boy. Oh yes, if anyone calls you a wanker, lad, they are trying to say you're useless."

Tea had already started when I got to the dining room. I sat down with still a red face.

"Are you ok?" said Randy.

"Yes he just told me off."

"Well your head is still on your shoulders."

I'd been in the school for about six months now and for most people it was a lot to comprehend; it was relentless, this was learning the hard way, no respite. One mistake was painful or embarrassing. No halfway house on this, believe me. I grew up overnight; this was jungle warfare and no prisoners! I had gotten to know everyone and settled in, I stopped feeling upset at night, I understood the rules better – I still never knew what a good wank was (I will one day). The end of term was coming up, "thank God" – I was so looking forward to going home. Mum had written to me once a week, keeping me updated on life back home. It was always great to get a letter from home; it was like a mixed feeling of joy and sadness. Sad that I was missing what was going on at home and great to get the letter. In a way – torture!

Everyone was buzzing on the last night of the term, after lights out as I lay in bed half asleep, when suddenly a pillow came crashing down on my face. I jumped up, my bed was spun upside down on top of me, it was so fast. I could hear whispering and bare feet running around, then as I scrambled from under the bed, about three boys armed with pillows jumped me! I shouted "help me" too late, bang crash smack wallop. I got back under the bed again, under a hail of pillows. They tried to pull me out, then they suddenly just stopped. I could hear bare feet on vinyl running out of our dorm. Suddenly the lights went on, the place was trashed, beds turned upside down and lockers turned over, Gary said the Barn Owl dorm had raided us. "We need to get them, but not yet, let's get our dorm straight first. Let's get them 15 minutes before it's time to get up, then they'll get it from Ogden." Later Gary came around and woke us all. "Get your pillow and push the inside to one end of the case so it gives you a better swing." We all crept down to Barn Owl dorm about 20 metres away. The light of the morning was just beginning to shine – this was about 5.30am – and we burst in on them, turned their beds over, pushed them out of bed, hit them with pillows and left – it was all over in seconds! No shouting, just a silent attack, but as we crept back to our dorm Gary stopped at another dorm, "Kingfisher"; he slowly opened the door. "Come on, boys, let's get this lot as well." And we all piled in. This time they were ready for us, the pillows were flying everywhere, and I got flattened from behind the door, right in the face, so we got out of there pretty quick. Just as we got back to the dorm Mr Ogden opened his door. "Get into bed quickly before he sees us!" But the beds had been done again while we were out raiding. Would you believe it, the first room Mr Ogden went to was ours; walking in, he took one look at it and said, "Everyone outside in the corridor and wait." The boys from the other dorms walked past on their way to the washrooms and poked fun at us. Mr Ogden came back out to us and said, "Right then, you like a bit of fun do you, boys? So do I, come with me to the shower rooms." We followed him and once we were there, he said, "Right then, into the showers with your pyjamas on; cold showers as well!"

"Come on, sir, this is not fair, what about the others?"

"Oh yes, I forgot about them, wait a moment." He called most of the other boys into the shower room. "You lot stand over there and watch this lot go through the shower."

"WHAT?"

"Well, lads, you did say "what about the others" – in you go then." So we all filed slowly in.

"Are you ready?" Then he turned on the cold showers, it was freezing. Everyone was jumping around, shouting and trying to hide behind some-one – it was so cold.

"Come out now and go back to your room to get dry."

It was good fun for the rest of the boys. We walked dripping our way back to the dorm. Then getting told off for making slippery surfaces, because of the water everywhere and we had to mop the floors as well. But, it was great fun and we were all looking forward to going home, so you could not dampen the day if you tried. The morning just dragged; everyone was buzzing. Finally, it was one o'clock and the coaches taking us to Hook Station had arrived. While waiting for the train to Waterloo I was feeling excited, thinking of what I was going to say to Mum, my brothers and my friends. I had so much to tell. I hadn't felt like this before; I was so happy to be going home. It felt like my birthday and all my wishes coming true at once! The train journey was long and boring, as we shot through stations without slowing down, people were just a blur standing waiting for other trains. When we started the journey, everyone was talking, jumping up and down, but by the time we started the slow down towards Waterloo everyone was quiet. As we pulled into Waterloo, I was watching the platform, scanning out the window or hanging out of the window. We could see the parents waiting, I could see my mum and before the train halted, we were all leaping off with our bags and running to meet the mums and dads. Mum gave me a big hug, I could smell her, most of us have a very strong sense of smell as kids and one thing is for sure, mothers give off a certain odour when you hold them. A feeling of safety, we all remember that smell, it's engrained in us from when we were born. It had been six months, things were different at home, the boys were bigger, the house had been decorated and we had a colour TV. I sat down with Mum and John, while I told them all the things that had happened at school. I was glad to be home, even if it was only for two weeks. "Stewart," (the only time Mum called me that was when I was in trouble or something was wrong) "I have to tell you something, John has moved in with us."

"Yes, is that it? Good, I like him, plus you need someone to look after you when I'm not here."

John put out his hand and said, "Put it there, son." It was my first handshake. He did try and crush my hand, but he was a man, I was a 10-year-old.

Tony came to the door with Steven. "Let's go over to the slope at Barking Creek," he said. I had only been home for about an hour and the jungle drums were working. My brothers were out with Dad's brother (their uncle's). Mum just said go on then, off you go and be back for six. This slope was about fifty feet high and a one in two drop; we used to slide down it in bread baskets and most of the time fall out at the bottom or halfway down; it cut you to ribbons. It felt good to be home again with my friends. Steven was alright, but he had a sister called Linda, who was a tomboy and used to follow us everywhere, we just couldn't lose her – we tried everything, but she was like a blood hound. We gave up trying and figured that she would get fed up sooner or later. We were a small gang, then my brother Mickey also started to hang out with us; he was still as mad as a March hare, but he kept his clothes on these days. We were over at Barking Creek, walking along the top of the bank walls of the river, trying to push each other into the mud banks, as all good friends do! Mickey was following right at the back, then after about ten minutes Linda shouted, "Mickey has gone." We thought he must have fallen in somewhere, so we started to go back the way we came along the wall. We looked everywhere. After a while we became concerned, we were trying to think of anything that would help us find him. One thing was for sure, he had not fallen into the Thames.

Tony said, "Do you remember the man parked with the boot of his car open, by the wall we sat on? He has gone too."

I told the rest of them to keep looking, as I was going to run to the Police Station. I ran as fast as I could, thinking that my brother had been kidnapped. As I bashed through the big old blue double doors of Barking Police Station, behind the dark oak looking desk stood the Desk Sergeant. He was in a light blue shirt with a black tie, he was a hard-looking man. "Hold on, lad, where's the fire?" I was so out of breath, I couldn't get my words out. "Slow down, boy, get your breath."

"It's my brother, he's been kidnapped!" And I told him what had happened. He picked up the black phone on the desk, called an Inspector and I then told him the same story. I couldn't remember anything about the man or the car, I just couldn't and the harder I tried, the less I could remember. The police took us back to the spot where Mickey was last seen and we looked everywhere. I remember feeling very sick inside. We had been looking for hours when the police took us home in their car. As we pulled up outside my house, Mum came rushing out and started shouting at me. "You were meant to look after your brother."

"Hang on, I've only been home a day, bloody hell, back to normal, I'm in trouble again."

Mum started to cry and was shaking. The Copper said, "We better go inside the house." And as he said that, who should come around the corner, as bold as brass and eating sweets.

"Mickey!"

He looked at us looking at him and I'm sure he could see steam coming out of Mum's ears.

"Where have you been, you little beast?" she yelled and Mickey's face dropped, his mouth fell open and the sweets in his mouth started to run down his chin. "Well?" Mum moved her face to within two inches of Mickey.

"I found some money when we were over at the Creek, so I went off to get some sweets."

I couldn't tell whether Mum wanted to put her arms around him and cry with relief or put her hands around his throat and throttle him. I guess most mothers and fathers have gone through that feeling, when their kids fall out of a tree or off a bike or lose them in a shopping centre for a few minutes. Parents come rushing over, when they've decided you are fine, they say things like "are you stupid, dumb or something?", "I have a good mind to give you a good hiding; you gave me a heart attack".

Mickey got dragged indoors, the policeman went off smiling, knowing someone was going to get it. Jerry and I ate what were left of Mickey's sweets and he was sent to bed for the rest of the day.

I only had a few days left, before I had to go back to school. Time was going so quickly; there was a change in the wind. I couldn't put my finger on it, even at that young age your gut feeling is active. It was my last Saturday and it was going to be different. Steven had a friend called Barbara, who lived across the road to us and she'd moved in just four months ago, so I did not know her. She was about thirteen, she wanted to come out and play with us and I wasn't fussed. We knocked at her door, and she opened the door in a nightdress that you could see right through.

"Come in, my mum and dad have gone shopping," she said, so we did.

We sat down in the front room, white walls with a tiled black fireplace (with family pictures on), a new looking second-hand sofa with two unmatching armchairs, but no TV, just books everywhere.

She said, "Have you ever seen a girl's naked body?"

I looked at Steven, who was sitting there with a big grin on his face, arms folded, and legs crossed.

"Yes, yours, Barbara," he said.

She looked at me. "Well, would you like to see me, Stewart?"

Not wanting to seem a fool in front of Steven, I said "yes" and felt my face going red. She came closer to me and said, "Open my nightdress for me, touch me."

I put out my shaking hands and just pulled the night dress open, I could see her little round breasts, about the size of two tennis balls. Then she asked, "do you want to see under my knickers?", but before I could say anything she pushed them down to the floor. This was my first sexual experience; I started to get an uncontrollable movement and a strange feeling of frustration and my mouth filled with spit. I feasted my eyes on this lovely body, then she quickly pulled up her underwear and said, "quick, go out the back door my mother is coming", so we shot out the back door and scrambled over the back wall. I can tell you, every time I closed my eyes that day, I could see her body and I'd get a hard on.

That night was going to be my last night at home, I would be going back to school on Sunday and Mum had packed all my bits away for school. She let me stay up till 9pm, but when I went to bed I just lay there; all I could see in my mind's eye was Barbara and yet again I got a stiff on. My brothers were asleep, so I started to play with myself; it felt good and then I felt this little sensation and I jerked. It went all floppy, it was over in a split second, but I'd had my first climax – I think. Now I understood what wank was about, it was nothing to write home about.

Sunday had arrived and it was time to say goodbye to my friends for another six months. I was off to Waterloo Station, to meet up with the rest of the boys going back to school. I was looking forward to going back and yet I was also sad inside, I had a knot in my stomach, thinking that I wasn't going to see my family again for a while. Waterloo was very quiet, it seemed we were the only people on the platform, 150 boys all hugging their mums and shaking hands with the dads. Like sheep, we all started to file onto the train as the first whistle blew and 'all aboard' was called out by the train guard. The train started to pull out of the station, Mum started to cry and that got me going too. This time, as we pulled away from the mums and dads it was different: they slowly disappeared. I felt bad all the way back to Hook Station, where the coaches were waiting for us. Arriving back, I would never get tired of the view as we drove up the drive, along the lines of redwood trees and the grand old house. A lot of the talk was about the Moon and that NASA was going to be sending up a man in space rocket Apollo 11 this year, in August some time. We were in 1969, TV had lots of stuff about the war in Vietnam and how many US troops were being killed every day. I did remember a big demonstration in London had taken place. The Beatles looked like a bunch of hippies, but most of us would prefer The Doors or Diana Ross and of course Elvis. Some of the lads at night had a small transistor radio; we could listen to Radio Caroline. No one would listen to another station at night. The first night back was not as bad as the first night, when I'd arrived six months before – for me, anyway, I'd resigned myself to it.

The new sports season started a few weeks into the term, and I managed to get into the football team, as well as the swimming team. I also got into a lot of fights again! If they had a boxing team, I would have gone for that as well. This was the price for being the youngest boy in the school still, being the youngest, though not the smallest, plus add a bit of ginger prejudice, everyone just thought they could kick me into shape! This was becoming too much for me, it was now the Seniors taking their turn, as they wanted dogsbodies. Before it had been the Juniors getting their status or pecking order, but I wasn't going to be someone's slave. I had a black eye every other day (I had a continuous one for about three months), I even got the nickname Patch. I never lost a fight during that time. When I say, "not lost", I see that means you either give up or if it was a boxing match, I would have been counted out or stopped. Things started to calm down during the next four months – this was due to everyone becoming fed up with trying to fight me and not winning. However much they tried to beat me, I would always come back for more, and they would also get hurt because I'd always land a few punches.

I wasn't very bright; I couldn't read very well, and my English was poor. This meant most of my academic abilities were, to say the least, very poor, but as for being cunning, shrewd or scheming, I was in a league of my own. I was equipped with survival skills beyond the normal. I think life equips everybody in different ways, not everyone can be top of the class or a great sports person. I tried very hard in class, but I just couldn't cut it, I was just a thick person.

At school, most kids have a crush on one of the teachers at some time or another. Well, most of us boys had a crush on Miss Baker; she was about 35, with a nice figure and she always had a smile on her face. She never lost her temper with anyone. At dinner times, teachers would have their meals with us in the dining room during the week – everyone wanted Miss Baker on their table. One day, in Miss Baker's class, I dropped my ink on the floor and I had to clean it up. At first, I was fed up and was groaning and moaning to myself, but as I banged my head on the underside of the desk, I looked up and to my disbelief I could see right up Miss Baker's dress. I started to feel warm, I could feel my face going red and at first, I looked away. I carried on cleaning the floor, but I needed to look again, she had no tights on, and I could see white knickers. I started to get a hard on, I was so aroused for the first time I could not stop looking. I just could not take my eyes off her legs as she moved from side to side, I felt that I wanted to do something. As I finished cleaning up the ink, she stood up and, walking over to me, said, "Stewart, why is it taking you so long to clean up that mess?"

"Sorry, Miss," I replied, but I looked as guilty as somebody with his hand in the cookie jar, with a big red face and a hard on, that must have been seen by the whole class as it stood out. Well it felt like it, but in fact, it was so small then it would have not even registered.

Miss. Baker said, "You best go to the toilet and sort yourself out."

"Pardon, Miss?"

"Go and wash your hands, boy."

"Oh, yes."

I got out of that classroom as fast as I could, trying to hide the lump sticking out of my trousers. After I'd washed my hands and put lots of cold water on my face, I went back to class and my face was still red as I walked through the door and across the room to my desk. I could feel everyone's eyes following me. You know the feeling when you just don't want to look at anyone and you want to get back to your seat, yet you want to shout, 'who the hell are you looking at?'. Most people just want the ground to open up and swallow them. I couldn't look at Miss Baker without going red in the face; I just couldn't stop blushing no matter how hard I tried. When you start to blush once, there is no way to stop the red slowly getting brighter and brighter, until you feel like your facing is glowing and everyone for miles around can see you.

After a few weeks I was ok around Miss Baker and life went on. The school was putting together a football team for the new season, I wanted to play, but most of the players were older than me by two years. I was good, so they put me in the team as the goalkeeper – that in itself got myself accepted as one of the boys and not a new fart anymore. It also meant the fighting had all but stopped for me; this was because I was the only goal-keeper in school and if I got into a fight I'd be grounded, which meant no football. For the first time ever, I had some protection.

My first game for the school was against Hellsey College, which was a match equivalent to Liverpool v Everton in a cup final. Over the years we'd beaten them more times than they had beaten us, but in the last few years they'd won four out of the six games. This match was going to be tough and it was a big talking point between boys and staff all week. When

Friday came, the big match was the next day and I couldn't sleep that night. The afternoon came and the Hellsey Boys arrived by coach; we had to meet them off the coach and shake their hands. The kit was two sizes too big for me, I had no gloves, no shin pads and I looked like someone from the 1950s – even the boots were old brown leather with nail in studs (two missing). I didn't care, I was in the team, I would have gone out topless! Sitting in the changing room having banter, laughing, being called 'Ginger' as a nickname, but not derogatively, felt really good. I can only think of the story of no man's land at Charismas in the First World War trenches, when all the warring factions came together for a moment in time before resuming hostilities. As we came out of the changing room, about 300 boys and staff from both schools let out a big roar, my hair felt like it stood on end. Oh yes, they forgot to tell me that every year it seems to turn into a punch up. It had been raining for a few days, so the ground was soft with a few puddles on the pitch. I got warmed up by running around and trying to look good in the heavy kit. Now it had started to rain, the kit was like a sponge and my top was around my knees – it felt like I was carrying an extra 40 pounds around. Just before kick-off, about ten boys from the other school stood at the back of my goal. I looked at them, they seemed alright, but then about twenty boys from our school came and stood behind as well and this was very off-putting. My mind fixed on to the game and as soon as the whistle went the ball was passed back to me. As I went to collect the ball, I felt a small sharp pain in the back of my neck. It was a small pea, fired by one of the boys behind me. As I looked quickly around, I saw the boy put the pea shooter away, so I kicked the ball off the pitch for a throw in. I then turned around, ran behind the goal and jumped on the kid, punched him in the head and ran back in front of the goal as if nothing had happened. Amazingly nobody saw me – I mean the teachers, the boys behind the goal tall saw it. Then a big fight started between us and two teachers rushed over and broke it up. Mr Jenkins came over. "Who started it?" The kid holding his bloody lip said, "he did", pointing at me. I just kept looking down the pitch, as we'd just got a free kick, from just outside their 18yard box. I heard Mr Jenkins say to the boy, "You mean Stewart, the goalie?" The boy nodded just as Danny scored at the other end and everyone went mad, jumping up and down screaming and shouting. As the ball was being taken back to the halfway line, Mr Jenkins asked me, "Stewart, my lad, did you punch this bigger boy in the face?" I just looked at him but before I could say anything he said, "You see me after the game, boyo." He then told all the boys to go to the side line and the teacher from the other school took the boy with the blood on his face to the first aid box. I was thinking to myself I was going to get a right telling off but Jenkins looked at me and winked. As he walked off, he had a kind of a skip in his step, I don't know why. I didn't have much to do for most of the game, we were all over them until about two minutes from full time, then one of them broke through and started charging the ball towards me like a raging bull. He was a big lad, more of a tank, so I ran out and spread my body at his feet; I took the ball, but as I did, he kicked me in the head as he fell over the top of me. I let the ball go, then another player came up behind him and smashed it, I threw myself at him too, but the ball smacked me right in the face and I landed in a really wet muddy patch of surface water. The four of us and the ball were sliding around; it was a free for all! Everyone jumped in, it looked like a scrum, I was in the middle of it and I must have been kicked, punched and sat on, but I managed to grab the ball in this bundle. All of this only took a few seconds, but it felt like a lifetime. I looked a right sight; I was covered in mud and I had blood coming from my nose and the top of my right eye. As I kicked the ball away, the referee blew his whistle for full time and our boys started to jump up and down, shouting and giving two fingers to the other school. Even the teachers were happy, they stood and clapped, saying 'good show' and really thinking 'we stuffed you lot'. We all walked back to the changing room to shower, but as I walked in, the boys from the other school who were shaking hands with our players (the opposition), grabbed me by my arms and legs. I wasn't happy about this, as they looked pretty pissed off with me. "Help me, lads, come on," I cried, but my lot just looked at me. 'Oh shit, I've had it now,' I thought, I couldn't understand why my team wasn't helping me. I was twisting and shouting, but they pulled off my football kit and I was as naked as the day I was born. Then they took me to right in front of the school dining room, where all the boys and staff from both schools were starting to sit down for tea. Everyone looked out of the windows to see what was going on, that's when they let me go. As I was so engrossed with getting away and the verbal abuse I was giving them, I didn't even realize where I was until I looked around, when I saw everyone looking at me buck naked, I ran away as fast as I could! I felt a right prat, everyone was laughing at me, it certainly was a day to remember. I didn't know the man of the match would be humiliated, a compliment I think, but I was man of the match, wow!

Over the next few months, we played a good few games of football and lost them all! I don't know why, but we lost most of the good players who played rugby as well. I was fed up with losing, but some of the players didn't care. I started Judo with Mr Ogden – he was a Second Dan – and I took to it like a duck to water; getting thrown around on the thick carpet was great two nights a week. I 'm sure some of the seniors enjoyed throwing us juniors around like we were rag dolls!

Most of my evenings were taken up with some sort of sport, even after doing homework, which we had two nights per week (known as prep).

The summer was coming and at the end of June, the school swimming pool would be open again. This would be my best chance of winning something for Stuart House. I was fast swimmer (well I thought so), but I'd have a lot of work to do convincing the swimming Captain. I was only a first year and most of the boys in the swimming team were years 4 and 5. The notice went up in the dining room, giving the dates for the swimming gala between all the Houses. It was going to be in three weeks, and anyone interested should see their House swimming Captain. Like a missile I went straight to him asking if I could be in the team. He took one look at me and said, "You're a first year?"

"I'm a good swimmer," I said.

"Ok, Ginger, see you at the pool after school tonight about 6pm with everyone else that wants to be in the team."

I was so excited I wanted to burst, I told Randy and John (they were in other houses, Tudor and York), but they just said, "They won't let you in, you're a first year."

"You're wrong."

"Your lot are training right now, not after school," Randy said, "not after school, they get time off today to pick the teams."

I went up to Mr Jenkins who was the Playground Duty Officer and I asked if I could go for swimming try-outs now for my house.

"You better get around there, boy, they must be over soon."

I ran up the stairs, grabbed a pair of swimming trunks and ran to the pool. As I rounded the corner they were just finishing. The Swimming Captain shouted, "You're too late." That hurt me deeply and embarrassed me as I looked like a keen fool. I felt about two feet tall and I wanted to give him a piece of my mind. Instead I just did what I always did, kept quiet, bloody coward I was! I really was so looking forward to doing something to boost my street credibility within the House. I looked at him with welled up eyes and 'you've stitched me up here' went through my mind. I was not finished yet, though – I had to think on my feet. The very next day the team sheets went up on the dining room wall and I looked down the list to see which boy was going to do the Freestyle. It was a fourth year called Tony Sharpe. I also found out that Stuart House hadn't won the swimming competitions in over five years and that York House had the best Freestyle swimmer in school, Simon Webb. Most of the boys would train every night in the freezing pool, I would go along to watch, and I knew just by watching them I was faster than both boys. Mr Jenkins was the Duty Teacher who oversaw the training sessions, I had to get his nod to go swimming with the team. The only way I could do this, was to work for Jenko (short for Jenkins) in the greenhouse after tea. This would mean that when he was at the pool side, I would be just finishing cleaning up the greenhouse. One of the many good things about Jenko was his philosophy, do unto them what they would do unto you. If I helped in the gardens, in his eyes, a swim after work would be a thank you. I saw Jenko in the main hall with the Headmaster.

"Sir, could I speak with you?"

"Yes, what do you want?"

"Could I work in the gardens after tea?"

"Why?"

Now I had to think quickly. "I like gardening, sir."

"Are you sure, boy?"

"Yes, sir."

He looked at me with an inquisitive eye, he didn't believe me for one minute and to be honest, I didn't even know what a weed was, let alone a dandelion!

"Ok, see me tonight after tea in the main greenhouse."

This was right next to the pool. So, I went upstairs after tea and put my trunks on underneath my shorts and I hid my towel in the changing room. Did he make me work or what, I was so worn out that I didn't even want to swim. This may not have been a very good brainwave after all. Around 6 o'clock Jenko said, "Could you finish up, I have to take the swimming, you best get your towel and I'm sure you already have your trunks on!"

I looked at him and my mouth dropped open.

"It's ok, Ginger, I wasn't born yesterday, if you want to swim that badly it's ok with me."

As I got to the poolside, all the other boys gave me a questioning look and a few of them sneered at me. No Juniors allowed at this training time; this was the unwritten rule.

Jenko called out to me, "Stewart are you getting in the water or not, or is it too hot for you?"

I think I understood what he was saying to me – I hope I did, because the pool wasn't heated at all. In fact, it was the coldest swimming pool I have ever been in; when you first dived in, it felt like your head was hitting a block of ice. To describe the pool, I would say it was twenty-five by ten metres and two metres deep at one end, going down to one metre at the shallow end. The diving board was low level, with a wooden springboard and about two feet off the ground. It had horsehair carpet glued to it and the only thing missing from the board was 'welcome' printed on the carpet. I dived in and once I got over the shock of the cold water, I began to swim up and down, slowly to start with, while the others started to race against each other. After about ten minutes, it was plain to see that I was in the way of the others while they were swimming. Most of them were from Tudor and York House, as the boys from Stuart House had already been and gone. Mr Jenkins called out to the two Swimming Captains, who stood talking to him for a few seconds. I knew it was about me, as you do, when you catch eyes glancing at you. For a split second it's a dead giveaway, plus added to that a bit of laughter as they turned and walked away.

"So, you reckon you're good, do you?" was directed at me from one of the seniors still in the pool; I never replied.

"Come over here," said Simon. He was the York House Swimming Captain. "Let's see if you are."

I got out at the deep end and stood waiting as the other captain picked out two other boys.

"Right then," Simon said, "two lengths of the pool freestyle."

I was not ready for this, I stood looking in amazement, not sure what to do or say.

"Come on, Stewart, get to the edge of the pool and show us how good you are," Jenko shouted.

I was so nervous in my black skimpy trucks and very white body! The two other boys were taking it with a pinch of salt, they were just messing about. Jenkins shouted out "are you ready?" and we all moved to the edge of the pool. I stood still, the two other boys stopped messing around and stood ready to go; Graham looked me up and down with contempt, which for me was like a red rag to a bull.

Jenko shouted to us, "When I blow the whistle you go, are you ready?"

I stood on the edge looking down into the water with only one thing on my mind: to win that race at all costs. It felt like forever standing there, my ears were like a bat radar waiting for the blast, my heart was pounding. 'Bang' the whistle went off and my body just took off, hitting the water my arms and legs burst into autopilot, all I had to do was breathe. I felt my hand hit the wall at the other end and as I flipped over and pushed away, I could hear the others, they were very close, I wasn't sure if they were in front or behind me; I needed more speed, so I kicked into overdrive. My hand crashed against the wall at the finish and my body rose up out of the water like a submarine coming to the surface. I expected to see the other two boys next to me at the finish, but to my surprise, they were only just coming in to finish two seconds behind me.

Jenko stood up and said, "Stewart, boy, that was good, now get out, dry yourself and get ready for supper."

As I left, I could hear the boys saying to Simon that they had taken it easy and not tried too hard, but the look they'd given me in the water at the finishing line said it all for me. They could not believe that a boy of eleven could win against them.

The word quickly went around the school, that I'd beaten the Tudor and York swimmers in a race watched by Mr Jenkins. I didn't get into the team that year, as the selection had already taken place; I had, however, won my race, proved a point and earned some respect! That year, Stuart House didn't win the swimming again, it was an uneventful year and most things ran along smoothly. I was beginning to understand my role in the place, as did most boys after six months. I was still thick, no change on that front. Then I received a letter from Mum, telling me that they were going to move to a new house in Barking, Essex. I was pissed off about the house move, it felt like I was forgotten. I knew I wasn't, but when you're miles away from home and the only way of communicating was by letter, once every two weeks, you do feel cut off. It was only a few more weeks, then I'd be going home to see the new house and the new man in Mum's life.

I had changed, I'd become more independent and confident. I'd now got to the point where I was no longer upset when I went back to school.

The end of term came around very slowly, we were at the last night before the Friday; packing was done, and my kit stowed away. Oh yes – dorm raid night again and everyone was excited, planning which dormitory to raid. The dorm we wanted to do over was Golden Eagle as they were meant to be the hard nuts of the upper floor. Nobody ever hit them, because anyone that went in, came out black and blue. They always raided everyone else, except Golden Eagle. We had planned to hit them, when they went out of their room to do someone else; we would go in, wait for them to return, then hit them very quickly and get out fast. This night we kept watch, and when we saw them leave to raid Hawk, we shot into their Dorm. We hit everything we could, turning over the beds, and waited for them to return. We heard them whispering and laughing softly like a pack of hyenas, then as they entered, we hit them with pillows, water and anything we could lay our hands on. It was a hit and run, a Gorilla-Raid more like, and get back to our dorm as quietly as we could. Along the corridor, Mr Ogden's door burst open just as we got the last person back to the dorm. Everyone tried to jump into bed and make it look like we'd not committed a crime, but some rats had hit us too – the place was wrecked!

The light went on and Ogden stood there looking at us. "Right, you lot, outside in the corridor, face the wall and do not move a muscle." We all lined up, as he walked off down the corridor and turned the light on, in the room we had just left. We could hear him telling them the same, then they all came out moaning and stood alongside us facing the wall.

"Right, you lot," Ogden shouted, "you've got me up, so I'm going to keep you up. The time now is 12am, I'm going back to my room to have a cup of tea and you will all stand quietly until I feel I can go back to sleep."

We just stood there for a while, nobody said a word until one of the other boys from Golden Eagle turned and said to me, "What are you here for?"

"We got raided."

"So did we, it was so fast we don't even know who hit us."

I had a little chuckle to myself at this. About half an hour later, we were told to go back to bed. Most of us just lay down on the bedding on the floor, as we were just too fed up and sleepy. It felt like we'd only been in bed for a few minutes when Mr Ogden shouted, "Come on, get your hands off cocks and on your socks, boys, it's time for all of you to get ready to go home today and give me a rest for a few weeks."

We started moving slowly, all of us were so tired. I made my way to the showers, knees bent, hands dragging along the floor and my towel trailing behind me. I got under the shower, without even taking off my shorts, I was so sleepy.

The day passed very slowly, then finally we were all off home. As we pulled into Waterloo Station, I could see Mum looking nervous for some reason, as I jumped from the train. She saw me and a big smile lit up her face. I ran up and put my arms around her; it felt good and safe, her warm scented smell made me feel happy to be home. I didn't even say goodbye to my school mates, this was normal, boys don't do that – do we.

We got off the train at Barking Station and took the number 87 bus to our new home. As we walked up the path, Mickey and Jerry were stood at the front door. It was an end of terrace house, with a driveway from the main road into the front garden; the entrance was a brick arch with the door set back. It was much bigger than our last house and as I reached the front door, my brothers said, "come upstairs and see your room, come on", then they dragged me upstairs to the landing. My room was about eight by eight feet, located at the front of the house. I was happy, I'd never had my own room before, then Mum called out to come down and meet John again.

Mickey told me that Tony lived right behind us in the next street, so I got out of my uniform and went to his house. Tony was in the front garden with three other lads.

"Hi Stew, how long are you home for?" he asked.

"Two weeks," I replied.

"We're off out now, I'll come and see you later – we're just going swimming," he continued.

I said, "I'll come too if you want?"

The other boys looked at each other, I could tell they did not want me to come, but before he could turn me down, I just walked away and went home.

I felt pretty sorry for myself, I must say. I walked around the area to get my bearings for a few hours, as you do, and when I reached the back gate at home Mickey called out, "How tough are you?"

"Well as tough as you can get," I replied and stuck my chest out.

"Come out the back."

In the garden were some of Mickey's friends sitting on the floor around a bucket of water. As they parted I could see a half flattened black cat – it had been run over by a car. I looked at it, my chest deflated, and I went as white as a sheet; this cat was not moving at all.

I said, "It's dead."

"No, look, it's still breathing."

The poor cat must have been in so much pain, it wasn't going to last long. The boys asked what we should do about it.

"We should put it down, it's in pain."

I stood looking hard at this poor cat in its last moments, my chest felt like it had a big knot in it and at that moment I felt dreadful.

Mickey said, "Well, you reckon that you're a hard nut, so the best thing for it, is to drown it in this bucket of water."

"What, no, let's take it to the vet," I suggested.

"Oh yes, how are you going to put it in a bag and get it on a bus?"

John and Mum had gone out.

"Ok get me something to pick it up with."

They brought me an old pair of gardening gloves and garden shovel, I put on the gloves, slid my hands underneath its body and it let out a soft cry of pain, which I could feel running through my body like a tingly shock. It went from my toes to the top of my head; I wanted to cry! I dropped it slowly into the bucket, it started to fight for the last moments of its life, there were a few bubbles and it was all over – it was a very profound moment. The power of life and death was not something I would ever want to experience again as long as I lived.

We took it to the end of the garden and buried it. For a few days after I was very much moved by the experience and I felt quite sick. Questioning myself, was it right or wrong, and to this day it still troubles me deeply.

Home life was very different now, John was with Mum and they were in love and all over each other. It was good to see her happy again and the boys saw him as a stepfather. I was too old and just saw him as a person with Mum and I felt like I didn't fit in anymore. It was strange this time being home, it wasn't like home.

It was a Saturday morning and the sun was out, Mickey and Jerry were playing in the back garden. They had lashed a rope to a branch between two sheds, so I called out "let's have a go".

"No, you're too big" was their reply.

"Don't be silly."

I climbed the shed and as they jumped up on the other shed, both of them said again "it won't hold you".

I grabbed the rope and swung across to the other shed. "Told you," I said, but as I swung back there was a crack and I went down like a ton of bricks. I hit the side of the shed, bounced off and landed on my back, knocked the wind out of myself and had my leg stuck hanging on the wooden three-foot fence. I lay there upside down on my shoulders, while the two boys fell about laughing.

"Shut up and come and help me off this fence!" And still laughing, they helped me down.

I jumped up and looked down at my jeans to see if there were any tell-tale signs, cuts and rips etc. The back of my leg felt a bit sore, so I put my hand to the back of my knee and felt a big hole! I called out to Mum, to come and have a look at my leg.

She told me to drop my trousers and as I did, she said, "Oh my god, Stewart, what have you done?"

I looked down at the back of my leg and saw a hole about four inches long and about two inches deep; it looked like a sad mouth. Mum put a dressing on it and took me off to hospital on a bus (the red ambulance) – it was faster than getting a real one.

This time, when I got to the East Ham Hospital, the Sister had a smile on her face and I didn't feel a thing, even when they put twenty stitches in me. However, I was laid up at home for a few days after, just watching the TV. I was fed up to say the least, then a district nurse came around to remove the stitches and it was time for me to go back to school.

It was really different this time, I was looking forward to it – as I said before; I felt out of place at home. You know, everything just goes on around you, whether you're there or not and you're just in the way.

I was back at school and I was now almost 12. I'd been home a few times, but it was the same again. I became more distant from my brothers, they had their friends, were out most of the time and had different interests. John and I became only nodding acquaintances. When I was at school it felt safe and I was back with friends.

There were also a few new kids starting and I was now a Junior Dormitory Leader – it had been two years! My first night as Dorm Leader was one to remember, I had three new boys, four troublemakers, two nutters and a very camp lad.

It was about 12 midnight, and two of the new boys started to cry as they were homesick. I wanted to go to them and say something, but as I found out, whatever you say doesn't help. Most boys get over the homesickness after the second night anyway. The first morning is always mad, the new boys don't know what to do and the older ones just take the piss. My first morning had all the hallmarks of an accident waiting to happen and it did. Dave Douglas, the biggest nutter in the school, was in my dorm. He never got into trouble with any of the staff, only the boys, and I was always getting him out of fights with older boys. This particular morning, he got up and walked around his bed to jump on Ron, a new boy. He sat on his face and let off the loudest fart I have ever heard in my life, it must have gone on for about 5 seconds. The other boys began looking through our door to see what the sound was, well, I was gobsmacked when Dave finally leapt off Ron and he did not move a muscle! We thought he had killed him, but then Ron jumped up suddenly and made a beeline for Dave; his face was red, and his teeth were showing like a rabid dog, I am sure I saw a skid mark on his forehead. Unfortunately, one of the other boys had wet the bed and left his sheets on the floor, Ronnie stepped on the sheet, skidded along the polished floor, flipped over, hit his head on the side of the metal bed and knocked himself out cold. Mr Ogden came rushing in. "What's going on?" He looked at me and I started to laugh. By now the smell of that record-breaking fart, that any schoolboy would be proud to own up to, had filled the room and it was foul. Ogden saw Ron on his back, groaning and told me to shut up. I tried but then he said, "smells like the drains are blocked again" and that was it, I was off laughing again and the other boys started to laugh too. I had to leave the room, I could not stop, I could not breathe and I was busting for a pee. Running down the corridor to the bog, I tried to pee into the urinal, but I couldn't control it, it went up the wall and down my leg. I just could not stop laughing, it was even beginning to hurt. I heard Ogden call out my name. I said, "I am in the bathroom, sir." I heard "right, young man" and when I turned, I saw Ogden standing there holding the red fire hose. "Stop laughing," he ordered, and I took a deep breath and held it. I was winning until Dave walked up behind Ogden and let one rip. That was it, I was off again, so Ogden opened up the small red fire hose and let me have it, bloody hell it was cold; I stopped then. Everyone in the dorm had to clean up all the water and Ron the new boy was ok.

After a few weeks he saw the funny side of things, but Dave was getting a bit harder to handle. Then one day at the dining table, he asked me to pass the tea, but as I picked it up, he leant across the table and hit me right in the eye.

"What the hell was that for?" I asked.

"You think you're such a hard-nut, don't you?"

Now, I had stopped fighting a long time before he'd come to the school, so he wouldn't know what I was like to fight, he would only know of my reputation. I told him, "In the boot polishing room after tea."

The word had gone around that I was going to fight the nutter and as I got to the boot room, about twenty boys had formed a circle. It went very quiet as Dave looked at me from the centre of the room and as I took my blazer off, he jumped me from behind. Silly me, I thought it was going to be a fair fight. I tossed him off my back, he took a swipe at me and missed. I grabbed him, he bit me on the arm – that was not one of his better ideas. I lost control then and picked him up off the floor, smashed him up against the wall and let him fall to the floor. I told him to stay there, but he came at me again, so I hit him right on the side of the head and he went down like a sack of spuds. It was all over, he sat on the ground in pain and everyone left and went out to the forecourt. I went outside, everyone patted me on the back, but I was feeling bad for hitting a mate. I went back to the boot room and said, "Come on, mate, I better take you to sick bay, that eye is closing up fast."

We went upstairs to Mrs Jenkins, who saw us coming up to the sick bay door. "Fighting, boys?" she said, as she looked at me over the top of her glasses. Dave and I never fell out again, but we were never the same sort of friends again – we were ok, but that bit of trust had gone.

That term went very quickly, not a lot happened, just good old hard work. Then, three days from the end of term, one of the boys, who I can only describe as a little shit, when to the Headmaster and claimed that Mr Ogden had sexually assaulted him. The first we heard about it was when the police turned up to speak to us. We all knew that Mr Ogden was a good man, anyone that had a problem could go to see him and he was also our Judo Instructor. A few days before this all erupted, Gary, the boy in question, was given the slipper by Ogden for doing something. To get the slipper from Ogden meant you had to have done something bad, as he never ever lost his cool. It's amazing how things got bent out of shape and stories made up: that man was convicted by the school! I remember someone said, "Well, one night I went to his room to see him and he put his arm around me." There were lots of stories like that, all misread. Most of us knew that if you were crying, because you were homesick, he would talk to you and send you back to bed, ruffling your hair and putting his arm on your shoulders like a friend would. The police spoke to Gary again and this time he admitted that nothing had happened, that he'd just said it to get even, but it was too late, and Ogden just left the school. He didn't even speak to anyone before going. The power of a child's voice can sometimes be catastrophic – they don't understand this, or do they?

CHAPTER FOUR

1972

I WAS NOW FOURTEEN and a senior boy; most of the last few years had been a corrector, building for the future. I was now an Officer in the Army cadets, and we worked very closely with the Royal Engineers in Aldershot. We were based at school, and every other weekend we would be off doing things and visiting the Barracks in Aldershot. I was a young officer in charge; most of the boys were one to two years older than me. This all came about because when we went on a training exercise with the regular Army I came through with the awareness and ability to outsmart the opposition and lead. But what I was doing very well at was the swimming – I had won everything for the last three years. Life had changed for me at home, though, Mum and John had got married and I was a bit put out about it as I was at school when it happened, and all that did was to make totally dammed sure, I did not fit in there anymore.

I did not like John much and we never spoke when I was at home and all my friends from home had moved on with new friends and I had changed. All in all, this (school) was now my family and home, I was safe and protected, a feeling that as humans we all should cherish for the short time we have the privilege to feel like that.

As seniors we got a few more privileges; like staying up late, plus we were allowed to go out on the weekend to Basingstoke. This was a good time to be a boy at this school, things were changing: a new Headmaster, new teachers and yes, some of the old teachers were still with us. We also had a new Night Child Care Officer, Murray, he was about six feet tall with red hair and a Scottish accent, and he used to be a Scots Guard. The first thing he said to us was 'Mess me about and I will remove your nuts and feed them to the ducks' – do you think maybe he was a tad OTT?! He also smoked like a chimney, the ends of his fingers were brown and yellow from smoke, but one thing was for sure, he played mean bagpipes, he was very good.

We also had two new teachers, Mr Mould and Mr Roy Royal, games masters. The only thing I can say about Mr Mould is he was bandy; you could put a basketball through his legs while his feet were together, and Roy was a very good football player, ex pro we were told.

That was all the new staff and, of course, there were lots of new "Farts", boys to beat up. Most of the first week is just sorting out the dorms and the seating at the dining tables. I was not going to be a table leader this year due to my falling out with the new House Captain, Paul; I knew he would not like being called a spot infested dwarf – "I cannot see why he took it in bad taste".

This was going to be a good year, I just knew it in my bones, I was already excited, I had been told I was going to be Swimming Captain and I was over the moon, also Football Captain too. That was not a great move due to the fact they had never won the Inter House football, a right bummer – but I would take being a captain of the Titanic or the Mary Celeste. I drew the line at being the rugby captain though;because the size of the other teams would have meant getting smashed. I was young and the other houses' team were mostly 16 and 15 big lumps, nickel dragging cave men. I wanted recognition, not being unrecognisable after every game in the medical wing.

Well, after the first few weeks, everyone settled down, all the new boys had been given a smack around the chops and knew their place, we all had our dining tables and this was a skill for which a good memory was essential – to be a good Table Leader you have to remember all the big eaters

THE LIFE OF A SCREWBALL

that you have met over the years and avoid picking them. My new Form Teacher, Mr Woods, a tall man, very upright and always well turned out, also looked after the snooker tables on the first floor, which I could now play on as a senior. We had two tables, one half size and one full size, all beginners would start on the small table and would have to win a competition to play on the big one. Most boys had to wait for a year until they were good enough to beat all the rest, but I won my first competition and was allowed to play on the big table as the youngest ever boy. It only lasted a few months before I was caught letting someone play on the table who was not allowed to so, and I was put back onto the small table. Oh well, that's life.

My first game as Football Captain had arrived, my God, I had to pick a team from the biggest bunch of misfits in the whole world! I put up a sheet on the notice board in the Main Hall, for people to add their names and I waited for them to make contact with me. The rest of the Houses had already got their teams sorted out; the other Captains were taking the piss out of me, to be frank. I had fifteen boys wanting to play and out of them, only four had ever played football before, the team Goal Keeper, i.e. me, the Right Back (Bob) who was five feet tall and five feet round, the Left Back (Ricky) who was four feet tall, with a big heart and but no brains. The two Centre Backs were brothers, Gary and Steven; I can only describe them as nutters; plus the ball was the wrong shape for them, they just couldn't get the concept of football. The Midfield players were the scruffiest and had personal hygiene issues that I'd never experienced before, but they knew how to play. Our Centre Forward (Ron) was six foot two, with two brains, one for the top half of his body and a not very fast second brain for the bottom half. Our first game wasn't too bad, we lost by the odd goal:15-nil! Our second game was better, we only lost by 13-1. Needless to say we finished bottom of the House League.

I was counting down the days until the inter House swimming races. We hadn't won the swimming outright in years, but this time I was going to make sure we did better at the swimming, than we did at the football.

This year I started to learn the trumpet in Mr Campbell's music class. If you were any good, you had to play in the school band and if you were crap, you still had to play in the school band! Simon and I were the only two boys who played the trumpet – he was very good, and I was crap. We had been working very hard with the rest of the boys, getting ready for the big day, to play in the assembly. Tuesday morning came, the big day had arrived. We were sitting in front of the whole school and when I got nervous, I got wind (it's an inherited problem, that has been passed down through generations of our family). I was sure glad that the hymn was Onward Christian Soldiers, as you would not hear me go off; we started to play and as predicted, I was farting along with the beat. Simon could feel it rumbling across the bench and he started to miss a few notes as he tried to hold back from laughing. Mr Campbell looked over at Simon, his face went red and then the music came to an abrupt halt. My bowels couldn't read music and as the hall fell silent, I let one rip. It was so loud, everyone looked at me, but I didn't bat an eyelid – you could have fried an egg on my face. At the end of assembly, I was told to go to the Headmaster's office, talk about blow your own trumpet! I stood outside the office thinking that as it's something I had no control over, he would understand, I hoped. I could hear him coming down the corridor, talking to one of the staff and my hands started to sweat. He walked past me, like I wasn't there, leaving his door open. "Come in here, boy," a deep voice called out. I walked that path that so many boys did all over the country at some time, the hair on top of my head felt like it was standing on end. "Close the door." He looked at me over the top of his glasses.

"Well, Stewart, what were you doing this morning?"

"What do you mean?"

"Well, it sounded like we had three trumpets going."

"Sorry, sir, I was feeling a bit off colour today."

"Ok then, I think you need to go and see Matron and get something for it next time."

"Yes, sir."

"Go on then, off to class." As I walked out of his office, I took a deep breath and I thought to myself that I'd got off lightly. As the door closed behind me and I looked up, standing right in front of me was Mr Campbell.

He had the look of a man who wanted to say, 'well done this morning' and then pat you on the head with a baseball bat. He didn't look happy, his hand shot out and grabbed hold of my left ear – I hate that, it bloody hurts. "You little bastard," he said, then came the left hook to the other ear and my ears started to ring. I could see his lips moving, but I could no longer understand him, then after one last pull on my ear he pushed me to one side and walked away. Some of the other boys stopped to see what was going on. I said, "Piss off and find something better to do." I had two red ears. Mr Campbell didn't speak to me again for the rest of that term and I never got to play in the band again, which I think was unfair.

The swimming races were due in the next week, I tried to recruit more boys to join me, but I only managed to find three others. There were fifteen events, so I put myself down for ten, Simon for four, John for one and Randy as timekeeper (on account that he could not swim). Most of the week leading up to the races, the other House Captains were taking the piss out of us. When we went training there were only four of us and they had ten each. Mr Jenkins said to me, "I think you'll win this, I am betting on you." The big day arrived, 250 boys and teachers around the pool, the sound of all those people made you feel superhuman. My stomach was starting to rumble, well, this time I thought it will aid me and turn the water green. The Headmaster stood up and everyone stopped talking. "Let's have the boys for the first race," he said, so I walked up to the edge of the pool. The only thing I could hear was a duck in the distance and then the 'bang' of the starting pistol. I shot off, just like a bullet from a gun, I was already trying to swim before I even hit the water. My body skimmed over the water and every time my head turned, I could hear everyone shouting. As I hit the finishing line and the race was over, I realised we had won. Out of the fifteen races, we won a total of thirteen and it was a new school record. All the Stuart House boys just jumped into the pool with their uniforms on at the end, it was great to see us at the top for a change. It was a fantastic feeling; you could feel the hair all over your body standing on end and just so much emotion. I wanted to shout at the top of my voice "yee ha, thank you, God" and we lived off that swimming victory for weeks. Next day in assembly, when they handed out the winners' medals and the House winners' cup, we sat quietly until the Head said "Stuart".

So, I stood up and started to walk towards the stage – "not you, the Stuart House Captain" – it got a laugh, but I felt a complete ass! Then finally he called me up. "Stewart, come and get your cup and medals for your team, well done." It was one of the proudest moments of my life to date! It's funny, we still got beaten at every other sport, but from then on, we always won the swimming.

Mr Royal had entered our school into the cross-country 'Run for the County', but we had a problem, as we didn't have a team up till now. At night, we would play football out on the forecourt under floodlights, and this one freezing night we all turned out for a game and got screwed.

"You're all going on a run, lads."

"Oh what!"

I didn't mind playing football in the cold, but running was another thing altogether.

"Yes, lads, follow me, we're only going five miles."

Mr Mould took our names and he was going to time us. We didn't look like Cross Country runners at all, but we set off out of the school gates, went down the main road and ran all the way to Hook and back. It was now getting dark and me and a few others were knackered, so we had dropped back from the rest.

At the main gate and about half a mile back to the forecourt, the others said to me, "We're going to get back quickly, coming?"

"No, I'm walking, see you," I said.

They shot off, disappearing into the darkness. Each side of me there were tall trees and the wind was blowing and rustling the branches. The night had closed in around me like a glove, my ears were whistling, trying to hear any sound so I started to jog. I had this feeling that I wasn't alone, the scream of a fox came from behind me and I began to run faster. By the time I reached the forecourt, I had overtaken the other lads.

"Seen a ghost?" they said.

"Yes."

I was now in my last few years. I became a final year Senior, had been given my own table as a Leader and I had Mrs Baker on my table as much as I could – the pin up girl! 1973 was a very hot year. The school had a real military connection, from the past and present. This was a new thing, a school Open Day, where they would invite parents to come to visit school and find out what we did. My brother Mickey, Mum and John came along, we had a helicopter land on the main vista and I was wearing full military uniform – plus my family were given a three-course dinner; it was a proud moment! I knew my time was coming to an end at this fantastic place and I was looking forward to becoming an Officer in the Army. I had been to visit Sandhurst – I was taken by Mr Jenkins as he knew the RSM. I knew this was my true path, but I'd also played football for Hampshire Boys and Chelsea FC and they'd contacted the school to ask if they could speak to me about a trial.

I wasn't interested, it was the Army for me. I was not a goalkeeper any-more but a centre back. This year, in 1974, Mr Jenkins put together a rugby team, it was the first school team in ten years. Mr Jenkins was now 64 and we found out from his wife that he used to play for Wales and the British Lions. We had six weeks to train and come up to standard, we were a right bunch of nuts – we all were well built boys and our knuckles dragged along the ground! Also, for the first time this year, a cinema was set up in the main assembly hall and we watched "Where Eagles Dare". It was fantastic, the only films I saw as a kid were at the Saturday morning pictures. When we trained with Jenko, everyone became very good at side stepping – it was a real requirement if you didn't want to hit a brick wall called Jenkins. Man, when he hit you, your whole skeleton would rattle.

We had our first rugby match coming up and we only had one last training session. Jenko said he'd make sure we knew what it was like to get hit by a Welsh train! He said, "Ginger lad, run and get past me." Me being cocky I went for it, side stepped him, or so I thought. He hit me so hard, my bones are still rattling to this day. The rest of the lads just looked sheepish! You know, we didn't lose a game all of that year – 12 games, all wins.

I had a lot of fun at school, not much changed over the next year, but I was still a long way behind in my schooling. A bit thick really, most young boys would have given their back teeth to do the things I did at school and my last few weeks were something to remember.

I had wanted to stay on for an extra year – it had been like home to me for six years, all my friends were here and the people that I looked up to – but I was told that I couldn't stay on, so we had a few parties and said our goodbyes. Most of us would never see each other again; I was very sad. I can only say that at the point we drove out of the school gate for the very last time, I left a part of me behind, for me it was a moment that made my heart very heavy. Tears came from my eyes, as I looked out of the window and saw the building disappear, along with last five years of my life.

Coming into Waterloo and looking for Mum for the last time, wasn't so much a moment of excitement but a sad one. My long-term real friends were all leaving me, as I was them, and it was a typical male goodbye. "See you mate", when I really wanted to hug my friends and say, "miss you all". Walking away from Waterloo, with my back towards the place, I had a feeling of dread and apprehension. I had some friends at home, but they had all moved on, and Mickey and Jerry had grown up. John and I were not on the best of terms. Mum was always full of love and beans. Getting on the underground train was really smelly and full of smoke. Everyone was smoking and as Mum smoked as well, she would light up too – it was like a thick fog. We were in the carriage where the guard who opened and closed the doors stayed and he stood next to panels at the end of the carriage. The panels were built into both sides of the carriage, with red and green buttons and a microphone enabling him to speak to the driver. He would go to the left, then the right, depending on which side the doors would open.

The train floor was a brown wooden grooved floor with cigarette butts. We got off at Barking and my clothes stunk of smoke. I never really noticed this before, maybe it was because I was always thinking I'd be going back to my home – Tylney Hall. So now I was going into this unknown world. As soon as I got home, things got thrown away, the school uniform and PE kit. Getting rid of the old and in with the new.

CHAPTER FIVE

1974

A NEW CHAPTER IN MY LIFE, a new beginning for me and my lost family.

I felt more alone than I can ever remember feeling. The first few days at home were, to put it bluntly, a bit strange. I could sense that John was unsure of me – that was understandable given that I hadn't been part of the family unit for the past six years. A week after I'd left school, Mum and John wanted to talk to me about finding a job. We all sat around the dining table.

"You need to get a job, to pay your way for food and items around the house. It costs a lot of money to keep a home running, so we think you need to get a job as a matter of urgency."

"Ok, I'll start looking tomorrow."

Then my mum said, "John has spoken to a friend of his and he's got you an interview next Monday."

"Oh, thanks, mate," I replied under my breath. "You do know that next year I'll be going into the Army, I've got my papers, I will be 17."

John then said, "good for you" with a smirk on his face.

Mickey and Jerry seemed happy and got on with John, Mickey and Mum seemed to be really close, as Jerry was with John. Jerry was very, very intelligent for his age and John was a graduate from university.

Monday morning came around very quickly and John, the money grabbing leech, took the morning off to ensure I got to the interview on time. As we drove along River Road, Barking (in a Green Ford Zephyr 1972 model), the place had a dirty smelly look about it; you could see the smashed windows of old warehouses and out of which, the only remnants of life were the pigeons flying in and out. Most of the docks had closed over the past few years, it was ghostly and sad to see this once thriving hub of Barking dying in front of us all. You could also see few people walking to work, where once hundreds of people would walk; now they were lifeless and grey. A soul-less man, with a flat cap, old grey suit and black boots was reading a paper as he walked. He didn't even look up, fag in his mouth and puffing away – he must have walked that road all his life, and I began to think 'is this what life is all about? Is this what can happen to me? This just confirmed to me that I needed to do better for myself. I am not taking anything away from that man, maybe he was happy with his lot, but me – no! We pulled up outside some big green metal double gates, with the name Store-mills across it. John said, "this is it, ask for the Foreman, Bill, he knows you're coming." I got out of the car and walked through into the courtyard. Most of the men were over by a clock machine, which was fitted to the side of a wooden type of shed, with 'office' painted in white stencil on the door. Punching or clocking in, standing watching them was a tall man with swept back jet black greasy hair, with a face shaped like a ferret and ears that Dumbo would have been proud of.

He shouted out to me, "Are you looking for me, Ginger? Go over to that red shack and wait for me."

After about ten minutes he came over. "Right then, Ginger, I'm the Foreman, have you worked in a sawmill before?"

"No."

"Have you ever worked before?"

"No."

"What the fuck have you done?"

"I've just left school."

"Right, come back in the morning at 7.30am, you can start, we'll give you a week's try out."

John had gone by the time I got outside, I had no money and no key to get back in at home. That makes you feel really wanted. So I walked the three miles home. Mum was out at work too, so I was on my own for most of the day reflecting on the day's events. I could not help thinking I had been well and truly screwed.

Mum was first home. "How did you get on, Stewart?"

"I start tomorrow, and I need some money to get to work and eat."

She gave me a pound and some packed sandwiches, cucumber and a brick called bread pudding.

My first day on the job, I had to get a bus at 0700 to start at 0800, I was so happy to be there, all my dreams had come true! I had on a pair of jeans, T-shirt and old polished school shoes. I headed to the office to pick up my timecard, to use this clock and get my safety briefing. This was it: Don't cut your fingers off, bring your own gloves to stop splinters, tea break is at the machine for 10 minutes, lunch is for half an hour and you go home at 6pm. Monday to Friday. Oh yes, if you die, we sack you! Sign this, it's for a sub, as I guess you have no money. I will give you a fiver for the week and we get it back end of week. Your pay is £50 plus a bonus, you could get about £100 a week.

"Come on, lad." Bill took me to see two old boys, who were sitting on two long buggies with timber planks on them. "Right, Paul, Mike, this young lad is here to help you load today."

"Oh fucking hell," Paul said, "that's our bonus down the crapper today then. Why do we get new kids first?"

"Just do as you are fucking told, mate," Bill shouted.

Mike called me across. "Go and get some gloves from the stores behind Bill's shed, they cost 25 pence. They put it on your tab and you better get a move on, the band saw will be starting up in a minute and we have to cut and plane 130 planks before we get any bonus."

Mike was ok, he looked a bit like Danny DeVito and always had on an old pair of white trainers, with an old roll-up hanging out of his mouth – that would last all day. I think his trainers were white, his feet were terrible, oh God, for days I thought the smell was coming from the river, as you knew when the river was at low tide, the mud would smell. Now Paul, he was a sad old man of thirty, every sentence started and finished with a swear word 'fuck this' 'shit that', he always had a fag in his mouth and it would last him all day too, but that was because as soon as he finished one, he lit another! Once he must have smoked a 100 a day. It must be a thing they do; he didn't take it out of his mouth for anything, food, tea, talking, even sex; if you saw Paul in the street you would give him some money.

As I picked up my gloves from the stores, I heard loud screeching sounds, like jet engines starting up. I could not hear myself talk, Paul was waving at me, like he was about to take off, I could read his lips, so no need to repeat what he said. Mike and I stood at the back of the bandsaw; as the planks passed through, we picked them up and stacked them on the trolleys. We did six hundred boards the first day, my arms were about ready to drop off, I could barely even undo my flies for a pee! I told Mum that night, that I didn't want to stay at this job, I was going to join the Army, I had always wanted to join the Army, it was me. I had splinters in my forearms, so Mum helped me to remove them and put some TCP on it. I fell into bed; I could not even eat – my body was so fucked!

A few weeks passed by and I felt so fed up with everything, home, work, having no friends, then everything came to a head at work when I was sent to clean down the sawdust container. It stood ten feet high, by fifteen feet long. The sawdust and chippings from the machines was dumped into containers via the extraction system, then at the end of each shift someone had to clean down the side and cover over the tops with tarpaulins. As I stood on top of one of the containers, someone started up a bandsaw, which meant wood chippings rained down on me from the extractor fans. As a consequence, I lost my footing, fell into the container, which was like quicksand, and with every move I made, the deeper I sank. I knew inside at each end there was a ladder; shouting was not an option because the noise was too loud. I tried to sort of swim to one end, but I went straight to the bottom, I started to panic, I couldn't breathe properly. Then something happened to me that to this day I cannot explain. I was lost, then I felt a presence, someone or something pulled me towards the side and my hand felt the rung of the ladder. I pulled myself out of that container like a ballistic missile, I got to the top and hung over the edge, then crashed to the ground, bouncing off my arse. I had sawdust in every orifice known to man, but there was no-one around to witness what had happened, until Bill the Foreman walked in and told me, "get off your backside and get that container covered, the lorry is here to take it away". When I didn't move immediately he shouted, "Come on, move your fucking self, you useless prick."

"Do you know what just happened to me?"

"I saw you fall in."

"WHAT!"

I felt this red rage come over me, I lost it, I jumped up. "SOD" the pain, I grabbed him by the arm and pushed him, slamming him up against the wall and punched his solid thick head (missing his long-pointed nose). He sat on the floor in shock. "You're sacked."

I didn't say a word, instead I walked over to the container, opened the rear doors and the sawdust flooded out. What I did do was clock-out and sit on the bus feeling sorry for myself – when I stood up, I'd left a sawdust patch on the seat. I could feel the sawdust between the cheeks of my bum as I walked home.

When Mum got home, I was sitting on the doorstep (still no key), thinking hard about what to say to her.

"What happened, Stewart?"

"I got the sack."

"Oh well, these things happen, I was going to speak to you about a job that has come up at my place 'Magnavox'."

"What's it doing?"

"Working as a trainee Tool Hardener."

I was interested.

"Come with me tomorrow to see Mr Spenlaugh, the Factory Manager."

John came home from work in a bad mood, he had hurt his back or his ego. I didn't speak to him much at the best of times, but I had great pleasure in telling him that I'd lost my job and had had a fall out with his mate Bill.

"What did he do to you then, smack you one?"

"No, I smacked him one and left him with a bruised ego."

John took a long hard look at me and for the first time I could see some anger in his eye, it shook him – he was not sure at all! From that day on, things changed between John and me, at every opportunity he would try to put me down in front of everyone, he had to prove he was better. He was a stocky 5'8" and I was now 5'11" and stocky too, but I had been a fighter all my life. He was a left-over hippy from the 60s with the ponytail as well! As for me, I was battling, but my mum seemed really happy. Although this was my home, I felt a stranger in it – so what could I do – just get on with life. For my interview with Mr Spenlaugh, Mum walked me to the waiting office; the room was half plasterboard and the top half was clear glass, so you could see straight into the factory. This place had three buildings, it was big, set on about three acres on the A13 in Barking. I sat in reception for about five minutes, until an Indian man walked up and asked, "Are you Stewart? I am Bill."

He sounds okay I thought.

"Come with me–" and we went through a pair of heavy rubber doors, onto a factory floor. We walked between two white lines, there were people everywhere, all mechanists, it was breathtaking and noisy. I could hear a radio playing over the loudspeakers, then we walked through two more doors and into a room full of furnaces, it must have been a hundred degrees. We sat down at a small square metal table in the centre of the room. He explained that there was a Managers' Meeting that morning, so he would be interviewing me instead.

"I'm the Foreman of this department and the Metallurgist, we are looking for someone to be trained up to take over when I retire. Let me show you how this place works, come on."

We walked over to a furnace with what looked like two melting pots, one looked like what I can describe as looking into a volcano with hot lava and the other one empty. As I looked in, I could feel my face melting!

Bill said, "This is where you'll be starting work, the others you'll get to know as you progress. This room stays locked as we keep cyanide in here."

"What for?" I asked.

"For case hardening around metal."

I already liked Bill, he was an Indian from East Ham, six foot five, with no hair and glasses. However, he had this habit: his two front teeth were on a bridge and he kept popping them in and out of his mouth with his tongue.

"Do you want the job?" he asked, and he didn't call me Ginger.

"Yes."

"Ok, I'll talk to Personnel and they will tell you the rest, come on then."

I had bit of a quick nod introduction to the old lads in the tool making shop. We walked back down the factory floor to a large room with half glass all the way round it, like a goldfish bowl, with milling machines and other tool making machines. I met a few of the men, most of them wore a light brown overall coat and one wore a white coat (he had the foreman blue badge above his pocket on his chest). We went off to Personnel, where they told me I was going to be paid £75 a week and I'd start on Monday. Only a few people at Magnavox knew that Gwen was my mother and for a long time some thought that she was cradle snatching, that we were having it off to put it bluntly, but I soon put everyone straight. It was a good job, Bill and I got on very well and became very good friends. After some time, I became suspicious of my mother; working in the tool shop was a tool maker named Tom; I got on very well with Tom and some lunch times I would play cards with him, if one of the other lads was off. He also knew my mother very well – I could never prove anything, but I knew something was going on! I don't blame her; she was very good looking and Tom made her laugh. Mum would go out for a ride in Tom's yellow and black Beetle, they would be gone for an hour or so. I dropped a few hints, but they were taken badly by Mum, so I wasn't sure.

Things were settling down at home, Peter and Joan had moved in just around the corner, I had not seen them in a few years; Gary, Martin and Debbie had all grown up and I started to go and see them every other day. I would stay at their house on the weekends. Life was going well, but I was still thinking of joining the Army. I had to go to Sandhurst to meet an

Officer of recruitment, who I knew from his visit to our school. This was in November, before my 18th Birthday – I was counting down the days. I also went down to the local recruitment office. As I walked in, I saw a tall barrel-chested man about 6′2″, wearing a battle green jumper with three stripes on each arm.

"Yes, young man, what can I do for you?"

"I would like to join the Army, I have papers from school to be an officer," I said. "Ok, you have come to the right place, take a seat and I will show you what the Army can offer you as a career." He took me through everything, but the one thing I wanted to do, was to be a military police-man. I was told to come back on the Monday to take a few tests, after that I'd be sent for a medical and then I'd be in. I told him I wanted to sign up for twenty years. For the rest of the weekend I was on top of the world, but I didn't want to tell anyone what I was up to yet, so I told Mum that I was going to be late for work on Monday and she never even asked why.

On Monday morning, I stood outside the recruitment office in London about an hour before it opened. This time a different, tall, upright man, very short hair, wearing three stripes (Sergeant) on his smart green uniform opened the door to me and said, "Good to see you, young man, come in. Tea, son? I've got some test papers for you to fill in, we have all morning."

After tea and a good old chat about how bad the Navy and the RAF were, he gave me the test papers to complete and they were easy! After I had completed them, we sat and talked about the role of the Police in the Army, as he felt I would be the right sort of person. I was told I'd be able to join in six months' time.

"Sorry?" I said. "Six months, why?"

"We're not taking anyone at the moment, but you are top of the list and we will write to you to confirm that this is the case. It will give you a chance to think about it and if you're still sure, then when we call you, subject to a medical, you will start training to be a soldier first and then straight into the Military police."

I didn't go into work, I was confused, I had been told I could go straight to Sandhurst, someone had lied to me – I was a bit gutted, I think! I hoped the time would fly, but the only person that would ever know would be me – keeping this to myself was a must.

Tuesday was a nice sunny day, Bill and I were sitting outside the furnace room talking about things – we often sat outside in the summer due to the heat in our room sometimes reaching 150°F. On this particular day, Bill was telling me about his parents, back in the good old days in India. All of a sudden something hit me right on the head, like someone slapping you with the flat of their hand. I jumped up thinking there was someone behind me messing about. Bill just started to laugh. I put my hand up to the top of my head and it felt wet – when I looked at my hand, there was a white yellow looking shit on it. A seagull with the biggest arse hole in the world had shit on me, it stank like fish. I had to walk through the factory to get to the toilets with this stuff dripping off my head onto my top – you know when you are trying to act innocent it seems to draw everyone's attention to you. It was like a chain reaction, once one person had seen me, the whole of the factory floor did, I couldn't get into that toilet quickly enough. The rest of the factory floor decided to go there at the same time and for days everyone took the piss out of me; I would have liked to get hold of that bird too and wiped its arse.

It was time for Bill to leave, he was due to retire, he had been a good friend to me, and I had an understanding with him. I have never had a problem mixing with people of all shapes, sizes and colours. It was Friday and Bill's retirement party was in full swing in the tool shop area. The Manager of the shop floor gave a speech saying that he was a good man, that he would be missed and wished him good luck for the future. It was so unfair for Bill, he didn't want to leave the job that he knew and loved and they could have kept him on if they wanted to, but he cost them more money than me at the moment, so cost saving etc. I knew what the Manager said was rehearsed bollocks, so I did one of those silly things that we all do and think afterwards what a dickhead I was: I turned my back during the speech! I think I thought I was showing some sort of protest, but I was wrong, and it still bugs me to this day, but you cannot turn back the clock. As I said my goodbyes to Bill that day, I felt the loss of a very good friend again. He shook my hand and I wanted to give him a big hug and say thanks, but this wasn't the done thing – a handshake or a pat on the back had to suffice. One thing that I was beginning to notice was, when friends move on, most of the time you never get to see them again or if you do it will be once or twice a year if you are lucky. It's maybe because we feel they shouldn't have interrupted our equilibrium, by having the audacity to upset our feelings. When a good friend moves on, a woman will cry or get upset and hug and show their emotion, but us men we do one of two things: either go out and get pissed with our mate and only when you're both slaughtered, say you are going to miss each other and blame the drink for your moment of weakness, or we start talking about the past, the good times and the fun days, not forgetting sex and football. It's our way of saying I'm going to miss you!

Friday night, most of the men/ boys of my age would be going out, I on the other hand had not yet made many friends in the area yet. I had one really good mate called Steven, who lived across the road from us, with his brother and parents. Steve was in the RAF, not as a pilot but as a mechanic. Lots of people who saw us together thought that we were broth-ers, as we both had red hair. As he was in the Services, we could go to the Servicemen's Club, meeting old boys from back in the day and talking about the war and other stuff, just reinforced my way of thinking – joining the Army Commandos was the way forward! Steve was home from Ireland, he had already been over there for a few months of his six-month tour; however, on this particular Saturday I was going to get my hair fuzzed up, it cost about six pounds for a perm. When I arrived home, Mum saw me and burst out laughing. She said, "I always wanted a girl." You know it can't be good when your own mum starts laughing at you – she said I looked like a red lollipop.

I also got myself a pair of white flares and black six-inch high sky-scraper shoes, not forgetting the black shirt. Oh yes, I was well ahead of my time for fashion! It was going to be the live music night at the club and Steve and everyone was going to be there. I was planning to get my glad rags on, but now I'd been shot to bits by Mum I gave it a miss. I'm not a confident person anyway; if my Mum thought it was funny, what do you think others would say? I was going to get a second opinion, but when I put my shoes on John said to me, "Don't fall off them, you will break something." That night I sat in my room, listening to Radio One and talking to Mickey about his dreams. He said he wanted to be an Artist. I was amazed as he didn't strike me as that sort of person, but who am I to make that judgment – I am still wet behind the ears, according to my Uncle Arthur!

This weekend was Mum's wedding anniversary and I was 'brother sitting'. On Sunday night about 8pm, Steve came over, to say he was meeting his girlfriend Sue and her two mates, Rita and Vivian, at the Servicemen's Club. Sue and Steve were trying to get me and Vivian together.

As I answered the door, he said, "You not ready yet, Stew?"

"No, I haven't got anything to put on."

"Just get a shirt and jeans on, mate, come on, hurry up, this is valuable drinking time going to waste."

"Ok."

I shot up, got changed and got Mum's key off her (yep, still no key). This is what friends are for, to put you in an embarrassing position. I liked Vivian and I got on well with her dad. Joe was a happy man, always looking on the bright side of life. Jamaica was his real love, he didn't want to leave, but his mother and father moved here on the Windrush ship in the 30s. His other passion was playing dominos on the weekends, sitting with others in the corner of the Club.

The night was not going to be a good one for me. It all kicked off about 10pm. As you know, by this time everyone has had a lot to drink, apart from me (I don't drink alcohol). The band started to play the slow dance – 10 CC's I am not in Love – and this seemed to be the moment all the girls abandoned their dancing with each other, to look around and see which gorilla was heading their way in the bad light. It must be a traumatic few minutes in a female's life, as they finish dancing, they grab their bags and rush off to the toilet, before they get grabbed! It must be some kind of ritual. I managed to get up enough courage to ask Vivian to dance, but before I could, some twit pushed past me and got in first. Oh well, I thought, that will teach me to be slow and by the end of the night, she was kissing and molesting this poor lucky man. All was not lost though, Peter and Joan were also in the Club and Gary (their son) came over to me and said, "Mum wants to speak to you about Lauren" – a cousin, she was not bad looking at all. I went over and Lauren was sat next to Joan. She looked at me with a smile that sent me a bit gaga, you know the one where the brain decides to make you look and sound a total prat. It must say something about us, when our brains can run our whole body until a woman comes onto the scene, then we go primate – well, I do anyway.

Joe said, "A girl has been sitting waiting for a handsome young man to come and ask her to dance, but she will settle for you and your new hair."

I could not even speak to her in the correct way. I should have taken up drinking, things would have sounded better. She was tall, about 5′ 10″, slim body and very well breasted. Her eyes were hard, they looked like they had seen hurt, no vulnerability, no quarter would be given if you ever crossed her. As she held my hand, it was the grip of a blacksmith – hard and firm.

Lauren stood up, walked over to me and put her arms around my neck. She started to dance, there was no music now and the lights were still on. A big cheer went up around the dance hall, I needed the big hole that everybody wishes for, in an embarrassing moment, to just swallow them up. The lights went down and the music started again, I could smell Lauren's perfume, it was 'Just Musk', it was my first dance with a girl up close, she moved her head off my shoulder, looked at me, she kissed me and this was the moment of truth after all that training on the back of your hand – hopefully it would finally pay off! My first kiss (without tongues) it was a warm soft feeling, I wanted more and more of it, for the very first time I felt like an adult. I walked her home at the end of the night, and we talked about silly things, about ourselves and hobbies etc. Her dad was at the gate waiting for her, I knew her dad Fred. He said, "if I'd known it was you, Stewart, walking Lauren home, I would have gone to bed. You coming in for a tea?"

I said, "Thanks, but I need to get home." I went to bed that night a happy man and looking forward to some good dreams, hopefully not wet.

Sunday 30th August 1975, Mum and John's Wedding Anniversary, they were happy that evening, they were going out with my uncle Arthur and Sheila for a meal. Mum did look great, she looked happy, long blonde hair with a flowery dress and a red belt with a gold buckle. She wore Marilyn Monroe red lipstick, and high heels, she looked stunning. This was the first time I'd ever saw Mum looking so dressed up. I told her about Lauren. "Good for you," she said and after they went out Mickey, Jerry and I put on the Captain Fantastic LP by Elton John. We were never normally allowed to play with the stereo, but tonight Elton John and his group were live at Ripple Road, Barking. I played the drums, Mickey the bass and Jerry on keyboards; we kept on playing one particular track 'You're Better off Dead' as it had great solo drums. It was a great gig and was one of the best nights we have ever had as brothers, we all felt together.

It got late, I had work in the morning, though the boys were on six weeks holiday still. I felt so happy, you know that feeling of bliss and contentment and it took me a long time to get to sleep. I was woken up by a bang on the front door, my bedroom was at the front of the house, it was daylight, the sun was up. For some reason I thought it was Sunday morning, so I leapt up and looked out of the window and to my surprise my cousin Linda stood there with a policeman behind her. I ran to Mum's room to tell her that Linda was here, but as I burst into the room no one was in bed, there was only a bunch of flowers lying on a bed. It was obvious the bed hadn't been slept in. It was then that a feeling of uncertainty came over me, as I rushed to open the front door in my shorts. Linda stood looking at me.

"Oh Stewart." Her voice was quivering and hiding something, her eyes had been crying and red. "There has been an accident," she said.

"Where is Mum?" I asked.

"John is round your Uncle Arthur's."

"Where is Mum?" I asked again, but she would not answer. I told her I needed to phone John, I slid my shoes on and ran out of the house like a bat from hell, round to Peter and Joan's about half a mile away, as we did not have a house phone. As I ran, I never once looked when I crossed road after road, I was fighting back the tears and I could feel a lump forming in my throat, I reached the front door and banged hard. Peter opened the door.

"What's up?"

"I need to use the phone," I begged.

"OK." The phone rang once and Arthur picked up. "Stewart, I will just get John."

"Why, what is wrong?" I asked him, then John's voice came over the line. "Stewart, your Mum–" his voice started cracking and getting higher– "I am sorry."

"Is she dead?" I don't know why I said that, but somehow I knew, then the phone went quiet. "Tell me," I cried down the phone, hoping, hoping I was so wrong.

A very quiet voice said, "Yes she has gone." My first thought was 'Mickey and Jerry are at home, I'll tell them'. "Are you alright?" I asked.

For the first time ever, he said something that meant something to me: "You're a strong young man, Stewart, and I got you wrong."

"I will see you when you are ready to come home," I told him and put the phone down. Then I just let go, it felt like my whole life had just stopped mid flow. I knew that John wouldn't be strong enough to deal with things and my heart was broken. I wanted to run away, is this a bad dream? Please God, stop hurting me, what have I ever done and at that moment my faith evaporated. Joan and Peter were lost for words, as I sat on the stairs, my hands cradling my head while I sobbed, I felt my body literally ooze pain. My soul was leaving me, and I was being emptied out like a bottle of water. Most people do not know how to deal with someone crying, even at the best of times.

Peter said the right thing: "Be strong for your brothers, they are going to need you, Stewart."

My brothers were still at home, innocent. I would have to tell them. I got myself together and walked back home feeling my heart turning to stone, as my mind's eye was watching Mum walk out that door looking so happy. When I arrived, the front door was still open, Linda hadn't told them, she was waiting for me to come back. The house was very cold and as I walked in, I took a deep breath. They were in the front room, on the very sofa we'd had so much fun on the night before, jumping around and happy – the scene of three brothers bonding. This was now going to be the biggest test of our lives. Mickey and Jerry looked at me as I walked through the door, their eyes scanning my every move to try to get some sort of idea what was wrong. My very soul fighting me emissions to be strong and say what I need to say and looking at the boys sitting on the sofa, the scared eyes and chins quivering with expectation. I looked at Linda, still hoping it was a bad dream.

"Mum has gone."

"Gone, what do you mean?"

"Gone, she has died," I said.

They started sobbing, I couldn't do anything for them at all, even though I wanted to hold them and be with them, I knew I couldn't, I needed to be in control. Arthur and John walked in with Steve (John's brother), everyone sat around holding each other, but it felt like I was watching a TV soap. I felt so alone at that very moment, I slipped out into the back garden and sat down on the step. I knew all my hopes and dreams were gone, my life was going to change, John was not the boys' dad, so how long would it be before he left us? Why would he stay, we weren't his real family?

I had an inner strength beginning to come through and I think that was the moment in my life that I lost any zest for life and became robotic. They call this a 'black heart moment', my life had been sent off down a new path and it was one that I had no control over. I decided that I would never let anybody get close enough to hurt me ever again, my mind and body just shut down, as if someone had pulled the plug. I stood up and walked back inside.

"Arthur, what happened to Mum?" I asked.

He said that from what he could gather and was told, it was possibly a heart attack, but until they did an autopsy, they weren't sure. The rest of the family came to the house and I went into work, to tell them what had happened. I knew Frank would be cut up pretty bad, plus Mum had lots of very good friends at Magnavox. I walked into the tool shop, I could see

Frank working away with a big smile on his face, he looked a happy man. When he saw me coming towards him, his smile dropped, he knew that something was wrong.

"Hello mate, what's up?" he asked.

"It's Mum, she died last night, I wanted to tell you before you heard it second hand. Now I need to tell Personnel that she will not be coming back and I will not be in today."

Frank bowed his head, his eyes were full of water. "Oh Stewart, I am so sorry, my friend, I don't know what to say." He was holding back.

"Frank could you put the word around for me?"

"Yes, what happened?" he asked.

"They think it was a heart attack."

"But she was only 37?"

I left Frank and went to the Personnel office. Rita was the Personnel Manager, she was about five foot two with dark hair, very good looking and had eyes that looked into your soul. The Nurse Jan was also in the office. I remember telling them that I was going to be away for a few days, due to Mum having died. Then they both started to cry; this was something that I couldn't understand at the time, I knew that they knew my mum, but you'd have thought it was their own relative, the way they reacted. I walked out of the office and made my way home thinking 'why us? did we do something bad?'. That bloody saying that people come out with, 'only the good die young', anyone who has lost a young one will tell you that is bollocks.

Over the next few days, it was difficult around the house, John and his brother Steve would go out drinking all day and the boys and I would sit and talk about Mum and how we missed her. She was not just a mum, but a friend as well, she would join in everything we did. Jerry was very subdued and quiet – Jerry was a very intelligent boy, beyond his years. He was a twin, but his brother died during the birth. Jerry could tell a great joke; his timing was always spot on. I don't remember even eating at the time. Mum just seemed to have walked out on us, as she'd left that night and hadn't come back again. We kept expecting her to come through the door at any minute, with a big smile on her face, saying fooled you all! We finally got told how Mum died – one of the main arteries into her heart had split and she bled to death. We were also told of the events leading up to her death; at about 9pm she had extreme pains in her chest, so John drove to Upney Hospital in Barking, which was two hundred yards from where they were eating out. They were turned away, because they didn't have an A& E facility, so he then drove to King George's Hospital about 30 minutes away. When they arrived, they put Mum into a cubicle and left her for an hour without seeing a doctor. When a doctor finally arrived, it was too late, and she died ten minutes later from loss of blood. Mum had been bleeding for over two hours, she bled to death and was in pain until the last minute of her life. We all hope that when we go, it will be peacefully. In reality, it's often not.

I can't even imagine what it must have been like for John, to watch his wife die in front of him and being unable to do a thing about it. I will never trust a hospital again – we expect to receive help there, not to be left in pain to die. My faith was tested to the point of destruction – fate is what dictates life, not your faith.

It was the day before Mum's funeral on the Thursday, 12 days after Mum passed. John and the boys went to see Mum at the undertakers; I didn't want to go, I wanted to remember her the way she was on that last night, with a spring in her step and a big smile on her face. I should have gone and said gooodbye, now all I feel is deserted. I was a coward and alone, it felt like I'd lost my very soul, like I was floating between light and darkness, a real lost soul – a ghost, that had no purpose.

That night, I had a dream that has never left me, and it sums up my life back then. It was a very cold day. I was standing in a trench with my feet covered in cool water, the night was very still, and you couldn't see a thing. I had a pistol in my hand, and I was dressed in an Officer's uniform. Suddenly, a flare shot up in the air and to my left and right I saw soldiers coming into view, hundreds of them, as far as the eye could see. They stood heads down looking at the floor, pushed up against the banks of the trench. A second flair went up, accompanied by loud whistles and everyone started to climb out of the trench, screaming "God save me".

I found myself scrambling up a small rickety wooden ladder, which led to my destiny. I ran towards the empty blackness, then all hell let loose, there were loud explosions all around us, mud and water smashing into us, then something hit me like a train and I fell down. I could smell the blood and mud that mixed around me, in this hole in the ground with a pool of water at the bottom. I couldn't move, I could only see and hear the sound of loud bangs and cracking overhead. The night went quiet and became very still again. I could hear men in the distance calling out for help or crying out for their mothers. As the night went on, the battlefield became ever quieter, as time slowly passed, then the moon came through the clouds, as if to have a brief look. The wind gently blew across the field like whispers, nobody will come this night. The rain started to fall pitter patter on my face and the light of the moon turned out like a light, as a cloud passed over. It will be daylight soon I thought, they will come to find us, the lost souls and daybreak seemed to frighten the rain away and the sun looked down on me with all its glory – a fine mist lay on the ground. With the sunrise, came hope, the air was warm on my face. 'Oh God someone come for me'. A voice called out, but it faded away and there was no more sound, even the wind was still now.

As the day passed, the sky turned red with anger, the sun was leaving me and setting, no longer able to watch over me, nobody ever came. I woke up alone that night, or did I?

The day of the funeral had arrived. Mickey and Jerry, my younger brothers, looked so ghostly sad, the loss of a mum at such a young time in their lives. You can never prepare for anything like that, we all expect our parents to see us grow, help us along and protect us. The funeral cars came to the house. I let John and his brother go into the front car first with the two boys, then I followed on after. I closed the front door, so many people in the street were out to see Mum off and there were so many flowers. When you drive that long journey to the cemetery, it's like you are in a goldfish bowl for everybody to see. Yet, we feel we should show our grief to all. Everyone sat very quietly, you could have heard a pin drop and Mum's coffin was at the altar waiting to pass on. My heart had turned to stone, I was not in that church that day, my soul was in hiding and not going to return until it was safe.

It was the moment of truth for me, she was gone, never to come through the door to call me screwball again. I could not give way to my feelings in front of my brothers, they needed me now more than ever. I looked up at the roof of the church and said to God, "how dare you hurt us in this way, you will not beat me anymore, I will never doubt you exist again, but I will never forgive you". I couldn't stay around after the funeral, I needed to get away from the crowds.

I could feel the daggers in my back as I walked to the car. Linda came over to me, she was so overcome with grief that she was unable to speak to me without crying uncontrollably. I put my arms around her, I could feel her pain and my body soaked it up like a sponge. Everyone started to go back to their cars, I saw my brothers walking out, scanning the people and looking for me. I stood tall, I had to look in control when they saw me, but inside I was screaming out for my mum. John had to be held up by his brother, this man was left with three young boys, who weren't even his.

That night was very hard for my brothers and I, as John and Steve had gone out to get drunk again. They came back about 1am and as they came crashing through the front door, I was sitting in the armchair. They walked through to the living room, John's eyes were focused on me (well they tried) and he said, "I don't like you, mate." I already knew that. "As of tomorrow, get out of my house."

"No, I will not, this is as much my house as it is yours, so piss off," I replied. He looked hard at me, I knew what he was thinking, but I was bigger than him and he backed off.

"I want you out by Friday."

"Oh, so are you going to look after my brothers then?" I asked and he said "yes".

The following day I went back to work, almost everyone avoided me at work, they didn't know what to say to me. Just talk to me, I thought, I need someone to speak with me. I felt isolated from everyone, I knew the first day back was always going to be the hardest and I was glad to be going home that night. I got to my front door and saw two matching black bin liners. I put my key in the lock, it didn't work! I pressed the doorbell, not a sound came from the house. I looked through the ground floor window and in the living room I could see John and Steve sitting watching TV. I banged on the window, they still didn't move, so I went to the bin liners and looked inside – my clothes! The bastard had kicked me out. Mickey and Jerry looked out of the upstairs window; they were clearly upset. We were still not that close, remembering I had been away at school for most of their young lives. John had been around long enough for Jerry to call him Dad. I should have seen this coming; Mum was the cushion between me and him; this would have happened sooner or later.

I had no place to go except to Peter and Joan, but they were away for a few weeks on holiday. Also, I knew that Peter would have come around and sorted John out – that would not have done any good!

One thing was for sure, you begin to find out who your true friends are in life. Now, I didn't have very many friends so to speak of and I'm not the sort of person who would force themselves on anyone at all. Some people can just walk up to anyone and be so confident, they could get away with it. We all know lots of people like that and some of us think we don't want to give a person the chance to say 'no' and leave us in an embarrassing situation. So, we go around the houses and give people a way out, so they don't feel bad about turning us down (or away in my case), even if we need help.

That night I slept on a park bench in Barking Park, it was bloody cold, and I only slept for about two hours. I had on about three jumpers, two socks, boots and a bath towel over me. One thing John did, was put everything in the bloody bags. I needed a wash and I knew the local swimming pool behind Barking Police Station had baths and showers; it would cost me 50 pence.

Carrying bin liners around with me got me noticed, that was for sure, I hid them at work, at the back of the cyanide stores as I had the keys. I did not want to tell anyone at work – what could I say? Keeping it from people was going to be hard, but as long as I came to work looking okay, it would be fine – as long as I didn't lose my job!

I kept to myself all that day, I never even went out of the office, still chilled to the bone from the night before. I needed a plan, but I didn't know what to do. I was really not looking forward to a night on the park bench again, I would have to find some place to stay, but I had no real money for a few more weeks, till the end of the month pay day. I had already given all the money I had to John to help with the cost of everything at home. At least food was not a problem – the work canteen always let us boys run up a tab until the end of each month.

That night I worked until 10 pm, until the Manager came in and said, "Got no home to go to, Stewart?" How true that was! So I walked round Barking until very late until the pubs had kicked out and everything was quiet.

I was making my way to the park, and climbing over the fence I snagged my jeans, great! As the Town Hall clock chimed midnight, the park was quiet and dark, only every so often a car would pass by, or a dog would bark in the distance. As I sat down on the old wooden bench, my eyes had become accustomed to the dark and I could see the outline of the trees, then suddenly I saw a figure in the distance, moving. I couldn't make out who it was, but he was heading towards me, about ten feet away I could smell him long before he reached me.

"Hello man," he said, "what are you doing on my bed?"

"Pardon, this is my bed," I replied.

He sat down next to me and the stink made me want to be sick – rotting fish mixed with an old rotting corpse! He had a bottle in his hand, a load of newspapers under his arm and was pulling a trolley. I couldn't make out his face and then he said, "Boy, I haven't seen you here before" (his voice was very gruff, with a thick Scottish accent) "are you lost, or a runaway from home, eh, boy?"

"No, I have been kicked out."

"Do you want a drink to warm you up?"

"No thanks."

"Well piss off and let me have my bench back, ok, boy."

I didn't want to start any trouble, so I stood up, grabbed my stuff and started to walk away. Just like I always did, not confronting the problem I guess, like a coward.

He called after me: "Boy, get yourself some newspapers, they will keep the wind out."

I was at an all-time low, I had been kicked out of home and now kicked off a park bench. I was definitely feeling sorry for myself that night! I walked alongside the lake, until from nowhere two geese appeared, making loads of noise. They caught me by surprise and as I jumped backwards, I fell straight into the bloody lake; shit it was fucking cold, it was only three feet deep, but I was thrashing about, thinking I was going to drown, until my feet found the bottom. For a moment, I had forgotten I could swim like a fish. I began to make my way to the bank but the geese started to have a go at me again, so I grabbed one of them round the neck to stop it making so much noise and he bopped me on the head. It was like the edge of a plate smacking me one – I was surprised! It must have woken up the whole park, I had geese and ducks going off all over the place and as I finally dragged myself onto the bank, a torch from nowhere flashed in my eyes and someone grabbed hold of my arm. "Come on, boy." It was the police. "What are you doing in the park – it's late?" (It was the wrong thing to say.) "I was moonlight swimming."

"We have a comedian on our hands, come on, boy."

I did not say another word to the officers, I just accompanied them to their van and sat in the back. I was soaking wet and cold water in every crack, bloody hell. Right next to the old drunk from the park bench, who said, "Hello mate, got you too, eh?" He was called Jock; well the police called him that anyway.

We arrived at the police station, and the copper said, "Come on, lads, out you get." I was numb from head to toe, it was like I was in someone else's body looking out. We walked through the back yard, into a light blue door with a small window halfway up. One of the officers banged on the door, another officer looked out to see who it was and opened it. He looked at us and told us to sit down on the floor "till the Sergeant sees you". After 20 minutes, a giant of a man just burst through the back door with four Police

Officers hanging off him, shouting and hitting him with batons. He was so big that two other officers ran to help, he saw them coming and he pulled back his arm like a battering ram and hit this copper right in the chest, the police officer flew across the room and hit the wall with a thud. The other copper rugby tackled him to the ground, they all piled in and jumped on top of him; it did look funny, all five coppers sitting on top of this lump of a man. They handcuffed his feet and hands and any other part of the body that moved, then dragged him off to the cells; the copper that took the full power of the giant got up and just walked away, like it was an everyday thing!

In came the top cop, the Sergeant. "What's going on, lads? Clean up this mess now. Who brought Smelly in again?" he asked.

"The new lad, Sergeant," one of the older hands said, with a grin on his face.

"Bring him to me." He looked at me, then looked away and shook his head; the young new copper came back to the desk and was asked, "Did you bring in old smelly for a night's sleep, son?"

"Yeah."

"Well, you can put him in cell number 2 and in the morning, you can clean up the sick and piss and everything that he deposits for us – you got that, son?"

He then turned to me and said, "Stand up, lad."

"Who me?"

"Yes, you, lad, are you drunk?"

"No."

"Then what have you been up to in the Park?"

"Trying to find a bed on a bench," I replied. I told him what had happened.

"Right, tonight, I am going to hold you in one of the cells so you can get a good night's sleep and we will give you a boiler suit that is dry, a cup of tea and would you like a roll? That is the best we can do from our canteen. I will also give you some addresses and phone numbers that will help you in some way, you don't have to sleep out on the streets. If you do, I assure you that 'Smelly' and you will become friends. Take him to cell 6."

That man restored by belief in humanity as I slept well that night, I was safe.

I left the station the next morning, I headed off to work hoping that I was not going to get found out. I knew the security guard (Duncan) very well, he kept his stuff in the furnace room to keep dry and warm and at night he sometimes would sleep for a few hours as the furnaces never got cold. I spoke to him, told him my situation and he said, "For a short time, why don't you stay in the furnace room, it's safe but on weekends you can't. Don't get caught!" I did that for about five nights, then at the weekend Joan and Peter came back and said I could stay there. Still not telling anyone – my stupid pride!

I tried to go and see Mickey and Jerry, but every time I went, that idiot of a man and his brother were at home. However, I thought my brothers were safe. I was becoming more and more used to living like a homeless person, living two lives, hiding from people and becoming more and more withdrawn; not wanting to speak to people. I had been away from a real home now for two months, I knew I had to do something about this and pull myself together. I had money but the phone numbers the Police gave me didn't even get answered. I also hadn't seen Lauren for about two months – she was off with someone else. I still liked her, but it was an ex-boyfriend that she went back to. I was happy to wait.

As I walked heading towards Barking from Dagenham, along Ripple Road, I bumped into Steve. He was home from the RAF.

"What have you been up to then?" he asked. I was trying to change the subject. "I went around for you last night and Mickey said that you'd been kicked out," he went on. "Where are you staying?"

"In the here and there."

"Why didn't you go to my house and see my Mum and Dad? They would have put you up until you got yourself straight. Look, I am just going to see Sue at work, come to see me later, I will speak to Mum, it will be alright, see you later Ok?"

"Yeah, ok." I didn't go to work that day, I needed somewhere to have a shower or a wash, plus I didn't have any money left. I thought my Uncle

Arthur might be at home, as he always started early and finished on half a day. I was in luck, he was in, so I told him that I'd locked myself out. I should have told him that the pig of a man had thrown me out as well, but as usual, I didn't want to start trouble. He let me have a bath before Sheila got home – for the life of me I don't know why.

That night I went to see my brothers. Mickey was out, but Jerry looked out of the bedroom window at the front of the house and said, "Dad said I'm not allowed to let you in."

"Where is the bastard?" I asked.

"At work," Jerry replied.

Then two police officers got out of a car and asked me, "Are you Mr Hampton?"

I said, "No, he is at work, why?"

"We have a Mickey Byrne down at the Station, will you tell him to contact us as soon as possible."

"I am Mickey's brother, Stewart, can I help?"

"Sorry, mate, just tell Mr Hampton to come to Barking nick."

I found out that night from Tony (Mickey's best friend) that he was done for breaking and entering. The rest of the family was falling apart, just two months after Mum's funeral – I felt so helpless. I still had no place to stay that night, so this time I knew if I went to see Uncle Arthur again, I could stay late and maybe he would even say I could stay for the night – but to my dismay they were out. It was going to be a cold night and I had left all my stuff at work. I was walking the streets again, but this time I saw people that I'd never seen before – or to tell you the truth, I'd never noticed before. I guess none of us see them, because we're full of our own importance. I started seeing drunks asleep in doorways, homeless tramps setting up box beds, and prostitutes walking in and out of the shadows as cars drove by. There were even some drug dealers standing on the corner openly selling, only going back into the shadows when a car passed by. This was all new to me, a side of human nature that someone my age would usually be sheltered from, unless you grew up in this world of despair.

It's like night and day, and I was seeing the night shift. It was about 2am and the night shift had all but gone, the roads were very quiet, a woman hooker, standing waiting for a punter, saw me on the other side of the road and called out to me, "Come over here, young man," which was a bit of a tongue in cheek comment, don't you think? I walked over to her, she was about 5′10″, thin, with what looked like dark hair. She wore more makeup on her face than a concrete underpass, big red lips and dark sunken eyes, she was wearing the smallest red skirt – you could spray it on – and a little boob tube (despite the cold), she was about as sexy as the Hunchback of Notre Dame.

"I have not seen you around here before, lost or something?" she asked.

"No, just looking for a place to sleep tonight," I replied, and she started to laugh at me.

"Next you're going to tell me that you're homeless."

"I am, as a matter of fact."

"Sorry, boy, I thought you were looking for business."

"What is business?" I asked.

"What's your name?"

I told her: "Stewart."

"Give me your hand."

"What for?"

"I'm going to read your palm–" and she drew my hand towards her and quickly shoved it between her legs. "That's my business, selling cunt, got any money?"

I pulled my hand away and said, "No."

"You're a virgin," she said, looking at me with a big smile on her face. "No, I'm not," I snapped back.

"I don't bite, well only if you want me to, come over here and I will give you a free hand job."

I said no thanks and she just seemed to turn on me.

"What are you, a poof, gay? Go on, fuck off, you bastard."

I was lost for words, she was still shouting at me when I was fifty yards away, her voice fading into the distance. When sex is involved, we change from lamb to beast in a split second. I headed to the Abbey Church, I knew a way to get in around the back when I was a kid, I could get some sleep inside, so I got in through the cellar door and found a heap of sacks to lie in. I was even past caring about one of my biggest fears, spiders – until I woke up and saw the biggest man-eating spider I had ever seen. It was just sitting looking at me, from its web, just two inches above my head, it had a big fat hairy body and very long legs. I felt all the blood in my head go straight to my feet; I had never moved so fast. I jumped up, hit my head on a wooden beam and fell to the ground in a daze. I glared back at this two inch round spider and stumbled out of the basement door with a big lump on my head; it felt like a golf ball! It was 6am, I had to get to work today before anyone saw me, I knew the other night watchman Dave would be unlocking at 6.30 and he would turn a blind eye to me getting in at that time. I got into the workshop without getting seen at all and I was able to use the shower room which was unlocked for use by managers. I retrieved my clothes from the cyanide store; I managed to do all this before anyone arrived at 8am. I knew it was only a matter of time before I got found out and then I would be for the high jump, no address, or job!

Over the next few days I stayed at the factory. I used to hide in the office until everyone went home and the place was locked up. I got food from the canteen and stored it in the cyanide store, it was safe unless I put the wrong salt on my food! It was ok for the rest of the week – until the weekend, then I couldn't stay, as there were guard dogs and men on site over the weekend. It was Friday, I had a bin liner with all my dirty clothes in as I walked out through the front gates and the security guard said, "Stewart, you got your washing?"

"I have as a matter of fact," I replied, and he looked at me sideways and gave me a big grin. "See you Monday."

Steve was sitting in his car just outside the gates. "Where have you been, mate, I've been looking all over the place for you. Come on, you're coming home with me tonight and we will get you sorted out."

I said, "I already have a place to stay"

"Yeah ok, I'll take you to where you're staying then."

"I'm ok, Steve!"

"Stewart, I'm your friend so let me help you. Come on just try it for the weekend and if you don't like it, then we'll talk about it; let's go."

Steve's Mum (Penny) and Dad (Tom) were nice people and he had a brother (Danny) a right little livewire but ok. I felt that I was intruding in their lives and I wasn't comfortable, you don't realise the words 'make yourself at home' are one of the most misquoted in the English language. I was to stay with Steve in his room on a blow-up bed; he was on leave from the RAF for the rest of the week. Penny took my bag of dirty clothes from me and put them out the back, Tom shook my hand and Danny just sat and stared at the TV.

The weekend passed by, it was good to sleep on a bed again and have a bath. I never left the house for the entire time he was home, so Steve and I got to know each other very well. It turned out that he hated the RAF.

He wanted to get out, but he had two years to go and he didn't have the money needed to buy himself out. He'd told nobody else, other than me.

Steve should have gone back a week ago and now he was AWOL; this was not a funny problem. Late on Sunday evening, Steve and I were home, but the rest of the family had gone out someplace. There was a rapid banging on the front door. I looked at Steve.

"Stewart, open the door, I'll go upstairs."

"Why?"

"It could be the MPs for me."

"You better go out the back door."

"No, they will also be out back."

Steve went on his hands and knees to the stairs and shot off. I opened the front door. He was right: two 6'6″ MPs with black armbands with the letters MP written in white stood there. "Are you Steven Knowells?"

"No, he has gone back to the RAF, why?"

"Well, he has not turned up back at the base. Are you sure you're not Steven?"

"Yes, I should know my own name."

"You fit the description we have."

"Yes, we do look a lot like each other, but he is 6′3″, taller than me, I don't think so."

He looked hard at me down his peaked cap. "If you see him, tell him to get back to the base. He's in trouble, but it's only been a week. The longer it goes on, the more trouble he'll be in, ok, son?" He looked me straight in the eyes. "Just tell him to be a good lad and get back to base." He knew Steve was in the house – he said it loud enough for the whole street to hear.

"Yep, if I see him," I said and they both turned away and walked back to a Land Rover. Two others came from round the side of the house and joined them. Steve came down when they had gone.

"What are you going to do?" I asked.

"I better go back and face the music."

"What will happen?"

"I will get 28 days inside, don't tell anybody." He went upstairs again and started to pack.

Penny and Tom came in and saw Steven's stuff packed on the stairs. "What's up?" they asked him.

"I've been called back," he explained.

"Why?"

"Just training, I leave in the morning at 6am."

I began to get my stuff together in my black bin liner until Penny said, "What do you think you are doing, young man? Look, sit down. Stewart, you can stay with us as long as you like, this is your home now, please just feel at home."

My feelings told me to go, but my brain told me that I needed to survive. I agreed to stay. Steve left in the morning, heading off to his fate and I was left in a new environment.

They were good people giving me a good home. For a few weeks everything was ok, I kept out of the way most of the time. I knew Steve had got 28 days inside for being AWOL. Danny the younger brother didn't like me very much. I never did anything to him, but I was not his big brother and I guess I was invading his space – but I took no notice of him.

It was Friday, and after work I decided to go and see my two brothers, as I knew that John would be out getting pissed somewhere. Then I saw Jerry going out with some of his friends. He saw me and he came over – I knew something was wrong.

"Stewart, Mickey has been taken away into care."

"What care?"

"I don't know, I know he still goes to school at Eastbury." I couldn't sleep all night, this man was systematically getting rid of my family and I needed to sort this out. I was up on Saturday at 7am, got dressed and went off to see John. I banged on my front door, the upstairs window opened, and Jerry's head popped out.

"What is up?" he asked.

"I want to see that prick now."

He disappeared then came back and said, "He doesn't want to see you."

"Tell him I will kick the front door in," I shouted back, knowing he could hear me.

The front door burst open and John stood looking at me with both anger and fear in his eyes. "What do you fucking want?" he asked.

"I want to know about Mickey, so where is he and what has he done?"

"Your little shit of a brother broke into some houses, got caught and when I went to get him from the nick, he didn't want to come home, so they took him to some place in Romford."

"Give the address to me," I demanded.

"Stay there," he said, as he walked away from the door. I followed him in, then he looked back and saw me. "I told you to stay out on the doorstep."

"Just tell me the address," I growled and continued to follow him into the front room. I was stunned to see nothing; everything had gone, the sideboard, the stereo, the new suite, the TV and video all gone. "Where is everything?" I said.

"Get out," he said, "it has nothing to do with you."

I was so fed up with him, I just walked away – I did not want to upset Jerry. On the piece of paper that John had given me, was a phone number and name of the home Mickey was at.

I called the number, but some man at the other end said I couldn't speak to him, unless I got permission from his care worker. I shouted down the phone, "I am his brother and if you do not let me speak to him, I will come down there and remove your spine!" I don't know what made me say that, I just lost it. He put the phone down on me and that was it. I went mad in the phone box; I was jumping up and down bashing the handset on top of the coin box and kicking out at the door. After a few seconds I cooled down and some poor woman outside was in a state of shock. As I came out of the box I still had the handset and I gave it to her and walked away. The look on her face was priceless, she didn't say a word. I made my way to Romford on a bus, to the Romford Road and I found the place. It was an old converted house with bars on the ground floor windows, with two lads stood outside having a fag, they must have been eleven or twelve. "Alright mate, do you want someone?" one of them asked.

"Yeah, Mickey Byrne, tell him his brother is here."

"Look, mate, they won't let you see him, but Mick is our mate. If you go around the back, I will tell him you are there, ok." With that, they quickly put out their fags, each took a Polo mint and shot inside. (It's only smokers that think Polo mints hide the smell of smoke.) After a few minutes Mickey appeared around the back and he looked different – his hair was sticking up, his face looked dirty, he pulled out a pack of fags. Was this Mick my brother I was looking at? It looked like him, I thought. I didn't say anything about the fags – I was just glad to see him. He told me that he had gone out with a few friends in Dagenham one night and got home late, then John told him he did not want him around and he was going to get rid of him. He told me that most nights he'd stay out and just go home to eat before going out again. One of the boys he was with, broke into somebody's house and nicked some stuff and passed it around the gang of them. He then got caught by the old bill and they all got nicked and banged up at Barking Nick. No charges were brought against them, but John never turned up until morning and he told the Police Mickey was uncontrollable, and he did not want him. "So, I am here," he explained, then we talked for a good hour until I went off home. I knew something had to be done soon, before the family was broken up forever.

Things were not going too well at Steve's house; I knew I should have said no to them. I had been there now about a month. Initially there had been no problems, but now the younger brother really did not like me. He started to show off and was making up stories; he told once that I'd said if he didn't let me watch a programme that I wanted to see on TV, I would hit him. That got laughed at by Tom, but I did start to feel in the way again; however hard you try, you cannot fit into somebody else's home life, even when they tell you to do what you like. Things like, you take the last drop of milk or you turn the TV over, or even though nobody is in the room, but I knew this was one thing that pissed them off.

Steve was coming home at the weekend; this was great – at last I would be able to talk to someone. He arrived home on Friday night and called me down from upstairs, as soon as he walked in the front door. His parents were out shopping.

"Come on, let's go out down the working man's club," he said.

"Ok, but what about your mum?"

"I have just got out of the nick and I want to have a beer and a bit of a laugh before I tell Mum and Dad, I'm off to Northern Ireland on Tuesday. I also need to spend some time with Sue this weekend."

We stood at the bar and Steve just got drunk;, he was still saying he wanted to buy his way out of the RAF, but most of all he was shitting himself about going to Ireland in the 70s, he really did not want to go. At closing time, we walked slowly back to his house. Steve couldn't stand up very well, and as I put the key into the lock the door opened and Tom stood there.

"What time do you call this then, lads? It's 12.30am."

Steve just said, "I'm off to bed" and walked straight past his mum and up the stairs.

She looked at me and I read her mind. "You got my boy drunk on his first night home and that is unforgivable." Regardless of the fact I don't drink, plus he was over 21, I knew that my days were numbered.

Steve got up about midday with a hangover, his mum was all over him telling him off in a nice way, like mums can. I kept away; it was an important weekend for them. On Sunday, Steve was staying at his girlfriend's house and that night Tom called me into the living room. I could tell something was wrong.

"Stewart, some money has gone missing," he said.

"Oh, so you think I took it?" I replied.

"No, I am not saying that, but only you or the boy could have taken it."

What could I say, game set and match to the brother and mother?

"Do you want me to leave?" I asked.

"I think it's best – don't you?" I stood up and said I would find some place to go, but what I wanted to say was: so you lied when you said, "stay as long as you like".

Joan and Peter had said I could live with them, so I shot off to see them, but they had been fighting again. She'd hit him with a litter bin, and he had tipped beer on her head, just another day in the life of Peter and Joan, but not a good time to ask if I could stay for a while. As luck would have it, I ran into Jerry out and about; he was looking scruffy, long shoulder length hair, clothes not ironed as usual, with a few of his mates. He told me that John had got himself a girlfriend and was not coming home most nights, leaving Jerry alone. I told him I was going to move back in that night.

"John will not let you," he said.

"He cannot stop me," I assured him.

I went back to Steve's house. No one was home, so I took all my stuff and left a note telling them I had gone and thanking them for letting me stay. What I should have written was a thank you for letting me think that you wanted me to stay, only to find some way of letting me go and making me look and feel bad. I think that was the only way they could live with telling Steven I had done something. They knew they'd made a mistake letting me in, although they should have been up front and told me I was in the way – I would have understood.

I moved my things back home, to a house that was 60% empty of furniture – he must have sold it. Jerry at least was happy to see me; he was only 11 and effectively living on his own. I had only been there half an hour when John came in. I was waiting for him. As he walked through the front door, he looked shocked. "What do you want?"

"I am back, and before you say anything, I am not leaving again."

He just said "ok" and walked past me. I was a bit taken aback. He went off upstairs, got changed and came back down.

"I am off, Jerry."

"Right, Dad, what time are you back?" Jerry asked.

"I won't be back tonight; your big brother is here to look after you." This was all he said before he walked out the door. Jerry was still the only one of us to call that slime ball 'Dad'; it had to be because he was so young when John first appeared on the scene. He then explained that John only came home in the mornings to see him, before he went off to work. He had given all the stuff that was missing to his new girlfriend. I went mad, I will kill him, I thought. I went upstairs to the bedroom that had been Mum's – there was no bed and the only rooms with anything left in them, were the other two bedrooms and the kitchen.

All my cup medals were even gone, I knew he was getting ready to leave big time! I took time off work in the morning, to see someone at the Council, as I needed advice. I met a Council Housing Officer and informed her of the problem, adding, "I think my brother and I will be homeless soon, plus I would like to get my other brother out of a children's care home." I could not believe how fast they worked, they made some phone calls to Social Services and they told me I had to come back tomorrow. I went off to work and spoke to my Personnel Department about what had happened, and they were very good about it. Especially as during all the late nights I had stayed behind, I had done a lot of work and was in front by a long way – production-wise. I got home about 6.30pm, the front door was locked again so I banged on it a few times. I called out to Jerry, I went around the back, but there was no sound or movement from inside. Then one of the old women from next door came out and said, "Stewart, a lorry came today and took the rest of the furniture away – Jerry went with John. I've got a key to let in the gas man tomorrow." She gave it to me. I went into the cold empty house, my mother's house and it was so bleak, cold and sad. I looked around for my stuff, and I found it in my bedroom with just my bed with all my clothes scattered as if I'd been robbed. I had – of my life!

There was no note or anything to tell me what had happened. My hatred for this man was growing by the second, now my brother was gone, and my life was going down the toilet. I stood looking around at the emptiness, then it came to me, I would no longer toe the line – fuck the world, I would do whatever it took to get what I wanted. I gathered what little of my life was left in a sheet (like a lining bag), closed the door and went to sleep on my bed for the very last time, in this – the remnants of my memories of my mother's home. It was a long night; I was hoping stories you hear about ghosts coming to see you were true, maybe Mum would come to me and tell me that everything was going to be alright. I just wanted someone to put their arms around me for one moment and say, 'I love you, everything's is going to be alright'.

First thing in the morning, I went to the phone box and called the Barking Council offices and to my disbelief they had keys for me to view a place in a block of flats in Dagenham, called Bassett House. It was a one bedroom flat on the 5th floor, quite nice and newly decorated; it was a tower block. I thought someone was looking over me (if you believe). It was better than a bench, or a shop doorway and there were other people far worse off than me. This is going to be the way I look at life from now on, I thought. I agreed to take it and I prepared to move all my stuff, on the same day that I signed for it. Tom from work came around with his van and helped to deliver my bed and clothes.

"Is this all you've got, Stewart?" he asked.

"Yes, but I will get more soon with my wages."

There were no carpets on the floors, only vinyl. Tom gave me an old black and white TV and I thought my new way of life will start – as of today. I am going to get the boys back together, we will start afresh and if anyone gets in the way, I will not be responsible for my actions.

At this time, the devastating lowest point of my life, I was now having to understand my whole life was going down a path that I had little control of. The ripple effect was going to affect my life's ambition of joining the Army – this now was not going to happen, and it was hard to take! My dreams dashed, killed off by fate. My football would be a way of some compensation, I was always being pushed to go to a semi pro club. My job was not what I wanted, and it had bad memories for me, with Mum working there. It was time to move on, never to look back from this day forward, and fuck the world. This was my place, my new home and our new start in life. It felt like I'd been on a real-life snakes and ladders game.

I still had very poor dress sense, my hair was all over the place and down to my shoulders, but I had a proud moustache!

CHAPTER SIX

1976

DURING THIS PERIOD OF OUR LIVES, it was going to define us, as to who we are today. This period in our lives was a mix of fun, hard times and sometimes bizarre moments.

I had moved into Bassett House, Goresbrook Road, Dagenham. The flat was a one bedroom flat in a 1960s tower block. You entered into a ground floor lobby, had a choice of two lifts or the stairs, and more often than not it was the stairs – the lifts just never seemed to work and stunk of piss! We were on the 5th floor, our floor had 6 flats: $2 \times$ three beds, $2 \times$ two beds and $2 \times$ one beds.

To enter into the flat, you turned left from the lift, through a set of doors and we were immediately left again – next to the bloody bin chute room. When you entered our flat you were hit by a dark L shaped corridor, the first door was a meter cupboard, then $5'$ on as you turned left again, the bedroom was on your right, the bathroom was just after (with no windows). Straight on by about $10'$ (to the end of the corridor) you entered the living room, which was about $20' \times 12'$. A window ran across the end wall and next to that was the kitchen. It had a few units in council green and a cooker left over from the 1920s! The views were amazing, Gorsebrook Park and the A13. The Ford factory that just seemed to stretch for miles, you could see the towering signs with the Ford logo on them and steam coming from some of the tall slim factory chimneys. The only furniture I had was one wooden armchair, with straps on the underside of a cushion and a black and white 20″ TV (with four push button controls), which had its pride of place in the middle of the room, sitting on three yellow pages books. The bedroom had one single bed, with one blanket, but no pillows. There was no carpet, only vinyl floor tiles throughout. The decoration was all cream painted anaglyptic wallpaper and of course I had no lamp shades, just a white pendulum with a bulb.

My first night in the flat was an experience to say the least. All I could hear was the lifts going up and down, people upstairs moving around, toilets flushing, but most of all, what made me jump was the rubbish chute. If you've ever lived in a tower block, you'll know what I am talking about!

You're asleep, then crash bang wallop, it's as if someone had just got a drum in your room and started bagging it for a few seconds. It was every few minutes, then a gap again. It was nonstop till about midnight, then it would start again about 7am.

I was now 17 years old, almost 18. I'd left a school that had a military structure to it, we were very self-motivated and independent – for survival. If I were a fatalist, I'd say that was a direction I'd been manipulated into, as that was life's way of helping me. Being left alone with no real help, no money. Forgive me for thinking that life has just fucked me over a bit, but hey-ho what's new?

My second night in the flat was a Saturday night and the lifts were up and down, the bin chute was going every five minutes and upstairs were just having a party. Next door came home around 11pm, and I heard them trying to get into my front door, they were too pissed to realise it was my door – somehow I drifted off. I was looking forward to going to work and getting some rest because of the noise, I was fucked, I really was. One of the lads at work told me that his father was a manager for Wimpey Construction and that they were looking for labourers – it was good money. He got me a phone number to call, so I called it. I was just told to pitch up at the site and "they will sort you out". I headed down to Dagenham Heathway, walked onto the new site and spoke to a man in the office. He told me to come back next week and see the General Foreman. I had the interview with a man called Pat Murphy, who gave me the job – "right then, you start next week". I needed the extra money; I had got to get my brothers back – whatever it takes. That was all that went through my mind at this time, it was the only way I was going to get my brothers back. I'd got a home and we could all live in together.

It was about 2am Sunday morning, 'bang bang' on the front door. At first, I didn't move, it must be the dickheads next door (pissed again) or the chute. But, the next time, I could hear a voice shouting through the letter box. I jumped up, looked through the peep hole, and it was Mickey my brother.

"What are you doing here?"

"Got out through the window, came over to see you, the home won't even know I'm missing. Is this place yours?"

"Yep and I'm hoping to get you and Jerry here. I've got to get two more beds, blankets and sheets."

Mick said, "I'll get them."

"How?"

"Don't matter, I got friends." He left about 1pm on Sunday and I gave him a key.

I went off to see Joan and Pete (my surrogate mother and father) to let them know I'd got a place of my own. I told them what had happened with Steve's parents and they got the hump with me, telling me off for not coming and staying with them. Anyway, that lasted about 10 minutes, as Joan cooked all of us a big fry up as always. Pete then took me over to his brother's place, they all worked for 'Rudge Removals' (cash in hand of course). They had two single beds that he wanted to offload, that were left over from a house clearance. It was Sunday late afternoon, a good drinking time, so Bob Crosby was in the pub. Pete and his brother would think nothing of downing about 10 pints! We found him standing propping up the bar, with a few lads smoking and pints in their hands. Pete had a few as well, before we all went off in his removal lorry, to the lock up around the back of the pub. We lifted up the back of the removal lorry to deliver the two new looking single beds.

"Let's go then." He jumped in the front, no worries about drink driving back then. They dumped me outside the entrance of my flat, with both beds and said, "we're going back to finish off our pints" then just drove off. My luck was in, Mickey was just coming out of the front of the building, but the bloody lifts weren't working again, so up the stairs we went! When I got through the front door and got into the bedroom, I couldn't believe my eyes – yellow sheets, blankets and pillows. Mick had a big smile on his face.

"How did you get them?"

"From the home, they have loads."

"How did you get them here?"

"On the bus. Darren, a friend of mine, helped me."

Oh yes, Mick decided to tell me that next week someone from the home was coming to see me. I asked why.

"He is going to let me stay here with you, they said I could stay as long as I had a bed."

"How did you know I was going to get a bed?"

"I didn't, we were planning tonight to nick two beds from the rooms at the top of the home."

"How were you going to get them here?"

"My mate's dad is a rag and bone man, so on the back of the cart, that would have been some fun."

The bed covers, sheets and pillowcases had in big black stencil BCC (Barking County Council). What I didn't see till later, was that the towels in the bathroom, 10 white towels with blue lines down them, had Barking Swimming Baths in bold letters. Looking back now, maybe the Local Authority did help without knowing.

It was now Monday morning and I had taken time off from my other job and walked to Heathway. It was about 6am when I left, as it was 2 miles away. The site had a big yellow hoarding with WIMPEY Construction splashed all over it and the site office was just inside the double gates. A big solid beer gutted ginger man with a voice that didn't match his size, squeaked at me, "What do you want, Ginger?"

"I have come to see if you need anyone," I said.

129

"Yep we do, Ginger, come with me."

We walked inside the office / portacabin. It had three offices, one at each end and one you walked through, as you entered. His office had a dark wooden table with two chairs.

"Sit down, son," he said. "You fit and well?"

"Yep."

"You look strong."

"I am."

"Well start Monday next week, ok, see me then."

I handed my notice in at my other job and they didn't say no – in fact they took it a bit too easily! I knew they were soon going to close down my department anyway. Monday morning come around very quickly, I got to the site at 0730 and spoke to one of the foremen.

I said, "I start today."

"What can you do?"

"Nothing."

"Hard work?"

"Yes."

"Go to the stores–" pointing to a yellow shed– "tell the store man 'Paddy' that I sent you to get Wellington boots, a shovel and a Donkey Jacket. Then, 'Ginger', come back here."

Well, apart from the fact that the boots were too big, and the jacket was too small, I looked good!

"'Ginger', over here," an Indian man called. He had a very strong accent and was hard to understand. "You are in our gang."

This was my first ever gang! I followed him and three other Indian lads, up along the site on a muddy and uneven track, that had dump trucks and forklifts trundling up and down all the time. We headed towards the main construction site, which was the start of a new shopping mall and car park with flats on top.

We got to an area that had six other Asian lads sitting around, smoking and just talking. It looked like they were waiting for something and I was right – 120 metres of concrete. It was non-stop – as fast as we spread it, it kept coming in. By the end of the day, I had blisters on blisters, pains in every muscle and my whole body ached, I wasn't sure if this job was for me! I had concrete splats all over my hair and face. Jit was the ganger's name; we never knew or used their real names.

Today, someone or some organisation would take you to task for bullying and racist comments. In his limited English, he said, "Ginger, you a good worker, back tomorrow." That made me feel good about myself, but my body was saying NO NO NO. I was coming back if I could get up! So that was my start at Wimpey, and it lasted for the next six years. This was a very strong path for me to take, it developed me as a person, my future was unsure, but I felt well equipped.

Today was the day of the visit from Mick's care home and the Council. Mickey was running around like a headless chicken and Jerry was over for a visit – he was still living with John and his new girlfriend some place.

The beds were all made and the flat was tidy, thanks to Mick. It was Saturday morning, which was also laundry day for us – all the week's washing was done in one day down the Launderette. For me and the boys, this became a weekly job and we'd have breakfast in the café next door, while the washing was being done and dried. Then back home again with all the bin bags. We never got whites, cos if we did, they'd never stay white for long – it was an agreement, no whites.

About 11am there was a knock on the door; four people dressed in jeans and shirts were standing outside, waiting to come in. They were all from the home.

"Bloody hell, Mick." Then they all filed in. I don't know what they thought about all the sheets and blankets on the bed and towels marked up with BCC. They only stayed for about 10 minutes and said, "he can move in".

The main man said to Mickey, "I don't suppose I'm going to get the bedding back?" Then he just walked out. He stopped as I was closing the door and said, "Mick can move in today if he wants." And that was it, no paperwork.

All that was left to do now, was to see if Jerry would like to come and stay too. However, Jerry was very happy with John; I don't know why but he was.

It was late Sunday, the day after the visit and I was just thinking to myself 'what I am going to do about Jerry' while Mickey was out getting his stuff from the home. There was a knock on the door, I looked through the old peep hole (as I always did), just to make sure I wanted to open it (as you do). To my surprise it was that wanker John – what the fuck did he want? I wanted so badly to kick the shit out of him, he was lucky that Mickey wasn't here.

I opened the door and looked down at this pathetic little individual and he tried without luck to push past me. When he couldn't, he just tried to big it up, pumped out his chest and give it the 'Billy Big Bollocks'.

I barked, "What do you want?"

"We need to talk about Jerry, he needs to stay with you, I don't want him with me."

"Ok, now fuck off before I smack you one." And for a split second I could see in his eyes that he thought about trying to take me on. Mickey come out of the lift with more bedding and Darren his mate. They had what looked like a load of tinned food and I mean loads! 30 to 40 tins of soup, beans, potatoes and tomatoes. Mickey was 14 years old, built very solidly and his feelings for John were as if John had killed our mother himself.

As he came around the corner from the lift, his face changed from a smile to hatred. He just dropped everything he had in his hands and went to go for John. I knew what was going to happen, so I just moved quickly and grabbed Mickey. As I did, John just said, "Good job you did that, I did not want to hurt him."

"Ok," I said, so I let Mick go. Mick was like a rabid dog. I don't think John was expecting this, Mick pounced on him and dragged him to the ground. As a man, John was stronger than Mick, but for a few seconds Mick got in about 10 punches. I then saw John beginning to recover, so I moved in and picked John up off his feet. He tried to push me off him, I just didn't flinch or say a word to him.

"Mick," I said, "go in."

John wriggled, got free, pushed past and was gone – never ever to be seen by me again, thank god.

In the flat Mickey was happy, he'd got some issues with John out of his hair and I was just looking in amazement at the food.

"Darren still has a key to the home, he got the stuff out of the kitchen and we've got more downstairs."

"Well, we'll eat well for the next few months."

That night, Jerry turned up with the universal been-kicked-out bags (black bin liners).

"John said I am staying with you for a few days."

"No, Jerry, it's permanent."

"No, he said just a few days."

"Come on, brov–" but he still wouldn't believe me.

After a few days, Jerry went to see John, or where he thought he would be – but he'd moved! Jerry told me what happened, he told me the front door was open, so he walked in and sat down in the living room, and he was then challenged by a new family that was moving in. The wanker had dumped Jerry too! But looking at it from a positive perspective, I had my brothers with me, and it was a new path that I was going down. I had a flat, with a new job, but I was still a virgin at 18. We will survive, whatever life throws at us and the time had come in my life, where I'd have to make life choices. This will be shown throughout this book. I would do whatever it took to make it work!

Now looking back, I feel at this point that my life had been heading down a pre-determined route. How do I know this? Because there is no other explanation.

CHAPTER SEVEN

The Flat

LIFE HAD A NEW BEGINNING for my family now and was a very memorable point in time. Elvis Presley died on 16 August 1977. The papers had it all over the front pages with his pictures, The Sun, The Mirror – in this part of the world, they were the only papers you'd see people reading. The news channels were showing his place in Memphis, Tennessee, USA, with crowds of people laying flowers and crying at his gates of Graceland. Over the following week the TV and papers just talked about how he died on the toilet, slowly building up to the big funeral with long processions of white limo cars, with police out on motorbikes and people lining the street.

Over here, it seemed everyone was playing Elvis music all the time, on car radios (if you had one) – this was the 70s, so not everyone had a car stereo. Car stereos were not fitted as standard and if you were lucky enough to get a new car, a radio was extra. Air conditioning, you must be rich! Cars around the 70s were great bricks on wheels, Ford Cortina Mark 3 and the Mark 4 were reps' cars, Vauxhall Cavalier for the working man, the Toyota Rust bucket was the cream. The Ford Capri was the young man's wet dream. This car was the bird puller, it was always the ugly lads who had one – with its long bonnet – it was a cool car!

Me, I needed a car, I was fed up with the buses and walking everywhere. It was not cool with the girls; it was hard enough being ginger to get a girl. I'd meet most girls at night, so they would not be able to see I was ginger!

God was cruel to us, when he gave us a pale body and bright red hair on top of our two brains. Naked, I had the brightest pubic hair ever; you could see me glowing from the other side of the room – thanks for that!

Our flat was very sparse for furniture; the living room had no carpet, one 32″ TV and an armchair right in front of it. We had nude magazines underneath the top cushion! We needed to sort this out, so I came up with a cunning plan. I had a car for about three months, it was on finance and for a first car it was good. It was a 3.5l, white Rover, it was an ex-police car. It had zips in the head lining of the roof and black rubber plugs where the blue light used to be. It was great to drive around in, listening to the V8 Rover engine, making a distinct sound. I then sold it and got £750 for it. I went out and bought carpet, furniture, a fridge and a lamp. The place looked great and I had enough left to get myself another Triumph 2500, a blue ex-police car from the auctions.

By the way, I never had a driving licence or insurance – who did? Most of my friends never did and if you got the old 'five-day wonder', this was the term for the 'produce your documents within five days' to your local police station, you went out that day and got a 21-day insurance, but didn't show up at the police station. Then, when they got around to chasing you up, go to another police station and just show the documents – then you were fine! No computers back then and normally you just saw a desk sergeant. By selling the car though, what I had actually done was theft, because it wasn't mine, but I never knew that. I got a copper banging on the door at 6am on a Saturday morning; he nicked me and took me to the Barking Police Station.

This was a new thing for me, never been in trouble before. My finger-prints and picture were taken, before putting me in a cell for what seemed a week but was only a few hours. I was interviewed and told I'd have to go to court Monday morning and I'd better plead guilty. They let me out after I signed the statement. Monday morning at 10am in Barking Court (I'd taken the day off work), I was told I could get sent down. I turned up in jeans, a jumper and DM boots, I looked a right head case sitting outside court number one. It was only a few minutes until I was called. Walking into the court room was intimidating – three magistrates, two men and a really old looking woman were sitting in the middle. I was shown to a seat in front of the bench; I went to sit down and was told "stand up, lad" by the copper.

The Clerk of the Court, who sat in front of the magistrates, said, "You have been brought in front of us today for the crime of selling a car on finance – that is theft. What do you say?"

"I did it."

"Why did you knowingly sell it?"

I explained the situation around the flat and my brothers and what I used the money for; I did not know it was theft.

"Right, what I am going to do is release you on bail for reports, I will see you back here in two weeks."

This was also being noted by the press. Before I knew it, as I walked out of court, a slim rat-faced man with a cap on, popped up in front of me from nowhere. "Want to make a few quid? Let me interview you about your situation, I'm from the News of the World."

I told him everything about Mum passing away and me currently bringing up my brothers. He gave me £50 and took a picture of me. Not bad! The next day we were on the front page of the paper, what a load of shit, I never said most of it and he even had a quote from the Social Services. They had no clue we were even living in the flat. My life was now open to everyone, but the only people who said anything were the lads at work. I was back in court two weeks later and received a passé very quickly. Three different magistrates were sitting this time.

Mr Stewart the Clerk said (I thought that was wrong, but you can't answer back), "You are in front of us today for non-payment of a fine for £750. How are you going to pay this back?"

I said, "I don't know."

"We set your payment at £5 per month, that is the order and you must pay it every month at this court. The court usher will give you all the information and provide you with further details, just wait there."

I was still in the court and I sat in the public area waiting for the Clerk to give the details to me. The next person up was an older man, in his 40s I'd say, he was up for not paying his wife maintenance. As the Clerk started to read out what the charge was, he just kicked off before he had finished: "I'm not paying that fucking bitch a penny, she was the one fucking my brother." He was snarling like a rabid dog and two officers just grabbed him by the arms – he got six months! I could still hear him going down the stairs to the cells shouting, "you, you're fucking wankers, you're on her side – wankers". Then, the next person got four weeks imprisonment for not having a TV licence for two years. I was still very confused, I asked the Usher what I was being done for; he said just non-payment of a fine, not theft. NO? Someone had obviously messed up the paperwork, so I just had to pay a fine.

I didn't want to be put away, I was still a virgin! See how a man's brain thinks? I was getting my priorities right. My brothers thought I was going to be sent down.

I was at the Heathway project, feeling very confused about life. I was walking towards home when a girl's voice called out from a car. It was Lauren, and she asked, "What you up to?"

We chatted, and I said, "Let's meet at the club, I haven't been there for some time."

"It's a date, see you Friday."

I knew Lauren, as I said before, she was the daughter of Fred and Kay. Fred was Peter's brother, they both worked for a removal company and were local hard nuts. They could be found, if not working, propping up the pub bar most of the day.

Kay was his wife, slim, very attractive (if she didn't have a black eye, that is). Lauren was a bit like her dad, a bit of a unit, not fat but solid. She could have been a prop in a rugby team! She was blonde with a 36 DD! I turned up at the working man's club, it had been a few months. Pete and Joan always had the same table, with about 20 other people. I saw Lauren, she looked very nice and she came up to give me a hug.

"Aunty Jo tells me you are a virgin," Lauren whispered in my ear. "Any time you want it, I will show you how." (She needed a few drinks first.)

Knowing the night was young and the fact that Fred and her mum were going to be at the club till late was perfect. We went back to her place; they had a three-bed semi with a wolf for a pet dog. Rex knew me, thank god; he would eat anyone that looked sideways at him. Fred and Kay never locked the house, and the sign on the gate read, "Trespassers will be eaten, and the remains prosecuted"!

We headed up to her bedroom, and I was thinking "what am I doing here?" – I really didn't fancy Lauren. We had been friends for some time, not good friends, but you know, seeing each other at parties and out with others. But I never felt the urge to kiss her or chat her up for sex. Also, she was out with a new bloke every other week. But she was a great laugh and an all-round good girl to be out with – as a friend. She could drink any man under the table; she loved a pint like her dad.

Her bedroom was about 6′ × 8′, with pictures on the wall of David Bowie and Queen, with a single bed and a teddy sitting looking at me from against the pillow.

"Get your stuff off then," she said.

I'd never taken my stuff off in front of a woman before (except my mum). As she took off her dress, her breasts just came into view and my cock just stood up like a rocket! She had no knickers or bra on. She sat on the bed, she put her hand out, clamped it over my shaft, she pulled me towards her and lay on her back. "Get on top." I sort of tried to climb over her, my stiff cock hitting her knees as I fumbled around. Lauren opened her legs. "Put it inside me then." I tried but my targeting was off, and I couldn't get in. She then slid her hand down and guided it into this wet warm place – it was amazing! Until all of a sudden, the dog decided to come right up to the bed and stood two inches from her face – looking at her – wagging his tail. She stopped and said in a gruff hard voice, "Rex, piss off, go on." What an off-putter, he turned and went out of the room wagging his tail, as if nothing had happened. She said "push", so I did like a rabbit. "Fuck me, come on, harder." She grabbed my hair and pulled it down. "Ooch!" Then she came, and her fingernails dug into my back – bloody hell it drew blood. She then pushed me off. *Was that it?*

"Come on, we need to get back."

I got dressed, I went home, and she went back to the club. That was not the best thing I ever had done – my hand was better than that! What a disappointment. It must have been me; I was just shit. Also, she left the light off, what, was I ugly or was I going to dissolve in the light like a vampire? Ginger people – they think we are averse to light, or girls never wanted to be seen with ginger men.

The very next day, I needed to go back to Lauren's house in the evening as I'd left my watch behind in her room. I got to Lauren's house about 8 pm; it was Saturday. I knocked on her door and Kay, her mother, came to the door.

"Hello, Lauren has gone with her dad to Wales to pick up a few things; they won't be back until Monday."

"Ok."

"Come on come in, I'm just getting ready to go out to the club later with Pete and Joan." She was in her white dressing gown. "I put the kettle on," she said, "sit over there next to Rex on the sofa." Bloody dog farted when I was sitting next to him on the sofa; it was rank. Kay just said, "Rex, get out, you stink." She gave me my tea and sat opposite me with loads of pink curlers in her hair.

"So, Lauren tells me you and she had sex last night." (I went red.) "It's ok, she tells me everything." I was glowing so bright; you could have turned the light off; it would not have made any difference. "Yes, first time as well!" Could it get any more embarrassing?

She looked at me and stood up and said, "I'll be back in a minute, just going to get ready."

I waited for about 20 minutes, then she came downstairs with her hair down. She stood in front of me and put her hand out and said, "Come with me, Stewart, I need your help."

I never thought what was going to happen, was about to happen. "Kay, what do you need me to do?" I was thinking I was going to have to lift something. "I'll show you, come on."

We went into her bedroom; I was looking around to see what was to be done. Kay turned and said, "kiss me", but before I could say anything, she just kissed me right on the lips, so soft, then she sat down on the bed – still holding my hand. She pulled me closer as she opened her dressing gown to reveal a naked body, that was to die for. Her breasts were small and hard, with nipples pointing straight out (like she was cold) and she was shaven below. Kay never said a word. I felt my whole body come alive, my mouth filled up as if I was starving, my cock was erect – so hard it was going to burst in my pants. Kay sat on the bed, her hands started to undo my shirt, sliding her hands across the top of my jeans, my body jumped with anticipation as my jeans were undone. Kay eased my stiff hard cock out and slid her mouth over it. OMG it was amazing, I was shaking all over – I was about to come. Kay pulled away before I did – "not yet," she said. I was naked and like a little novice. I lay next to her, my hands ran all over her body like I was mapping it – like a blind man. I felt every part of her body was moving, as her hands played between her legs. She whispered to me, "lick me, lick me". I slid down her body, kissing around the top of her and she moved her hands to the top of my head pushing me down. My tongue slid between her wet soft lips moving my head up and down, finding the right place, as she said "harder" and then she gripped my head and held me still as her body just shook and jarred, she screamed "yes yes yes! Oh Fuck! Oh God! Mmmmm."

"Come up here." She kissed me on the lips, I was being moved around. I was lying on my back now, as she got on top and softly placed my cock inside her. Only my hands were moving over her breasts as her body moved back and forward with me inside her; she was so wet it felt amazing. She grabbed me again as her body shook with pleasure; as she did I just uncontrollably started to shake myself. She said, "Don't come inside me." She jumped off but I was gone too far; Kay just got her mouth over me and took it all in her mouth. I grabbed the pillow and screamed with pleasure into the pillow. Kay came up next to me and said, "Hold me, Stewart, hold me." I did, we just lay next to each other, I was caressing her hair and holding her. We lay together for about two hours, it was late, about 1 am. She suddenly slid down my body and started to suck me again, bloody hell – it was so, so good. She turned her body round and straddled over my head and dropped herself onto my mouth, as my tongue started to lick along her lips. I could taste her; it was so nice as I could feel her body start to move with my tongue. Feeling her tongue sliding up and down on my shaft, she started to flood into my mouth, as she started to come in my mouth. She let go – "I am coming, I am coming," she screamed. She turned around, sat on top and said, "Come inside, come inside." She moved, she was in charge as she was, I came inside her. What a feeling of pleasure, my body was uncontrollable, both of us coming at the same time.

What a night. It was now about 5 am and she whispered, "This will never happen again, Stewart, promise me you will never tell anyone ever." I kissed her in the morning, and she said, "You are a natural, I could do this all the time with you, but it cannot ever happen, please don't say anything." Her eyes were filled with tears. I gave her a hug and left, walking home with the biggest smile on my face. Till this day, I have never told a soul. However, if you think I have just done so in this book you are wrong – I will take her real name to my grave.

Heading home, I saw all the preparations for the Queen's Silver Jubilee, bunting was up, and the people were getting ready for street parties it, was everywhere. You could buy plates, mugs, flags, every bloody thing. There was a good mood around the whole country and the TV was full of it too.

We had settled into the flat now and although we were all crammed in with both Jerry and Mickey, I thought we needed to get a dog – yes, a dog.

I was told that we could get the dog we wanted from Battersea Dogs Home. So, we all set off on this Friday morning, me taking time off work and the two boys were on half term. We got a train to Battersea. They showed us around; there were so many dogs, but one stood out to me. It was a wolf looking dog, an ex-security dog. They said it needed a strong hand. That was it, this was the dog for us (a frigging bear) so we took him. This dog was about waist high, his head was as big as a bear. As we walked through London, "Monster dog" was happily walking along, till a man on a bike come past too close. He leapt on him, dragging me along with him, knocking him off his bike and sent him spiralling into the road. He stood up, looking shocked, just got back on his bike and rode off. He kept looking back at this dog, who was wanting to eat him, with me hanging off the back of it, while both my brothers were falling about laughing. We kept on walking until we got to a pub and we sat outside. We called him Bear. He just sat next to me like butter wouldn't melt in his mouth, and we sat having a drink (not alcohol), with a bowl of water for the dog.

A man was running for a bus I think, I saw him out of the corner of my eye, but it was too late; the dog launched himself at him and he took me and the table and the man crashing to the ground! The man who was wearing a suit and had a fag still in his mouth said, "Get that fucking dog under control."

"Sorry," I said. We had to take him back before he really did eat someone. The sad thing was, he was most likely going to be put down. I was so gutted. I felt like I'd let everyone down at the dogs' home. We then chose a black Labrador instead, another right choice for the flat, he was about 8 months old and was full of life. We got him home in one piece and we named him Blackie. (This was not racist; it was because of his colour.) The next morning Blackie was not well, he had shit all over the place. The flat and the hallway stank. I found this out when I got up on Saturday morning and walked in it. Up between my toes, it was! I took him to the RSPCA, and they told me he had distemper, they gave him a jab, but they also said he may not survive the night.

This was very bad news and I felt so sorry for the dog so let him sleep at the bottom of my bed that night. On Sunday morning, he had passed away in the night. He was cold and stiff.

Jerry and I put him on the floor. Mickey just said, "Let's stick him down the rubbish chute." We could not take him to the RSPCA, because we had no car, so we would have had to get him on the bus.

We put him in a potato sack that we had left over from when I moved in. The chute is a funny contraption. You pull the handle towards you and it opens a V Shape drawer, just big enough to stick a large bag of rubbish in, then you close it and let it fall. However, we had a dog that was stiff and large, and we were unable to bend him. We were trying to feed him into the chute, as one of the neighbours from our landing walked into the chute room.

"What the fucking hell are you doing?"

It looked funny: Jerry was holding the drawer open, Mickey was feeding the sack in and I was holding the back legs. Whatever we did, he would not fit through. We took him down across the road, to the multi-storey garages and placed him in a garage that we knew the council always cleaned out once a day.

There was a problem at this time, though: a little girl had gone missing from Heathway Dagenham; it was all over the papers and police were everywhere, including volunteers.

On Monday morning, as I walked out the front entrance on my way to work, I saw police officers talking to people. Apparently, the Council workers had thought they had found the missing girl in the garages, but it turned out to be a dog. Shit, I was off – another close encounter with the Old Bill.

Over the next few months, I got to know about the building industry and the sort of people who work in it. It wasn't like how today's health and safety was done, but in its own way. Safety helmets, working at height and eye protection was not even thought of. Maybe that is why there were so many accidents and deaths in the industry. I was assigned to a concrete gang, I was the only Ginger; it was a gang of six and Jit (an Eastham lad) was ganger, the other lads were from Kentish Town. The building industry has always been a real mixing pot of all walks of life, always has been.

To be honest, I never in all the years saw much prejudice (only against Managers, everyone hated managers). I had not planned my life to be in the construction industry, but the money was good. Most people who wanted a job, could just pitch up anywhere on site or factory and ask for a job. If they needed someone you would get a go.

The site was a shopping centre, with flats on top. Wimpey Construction was the company I worked for. The site consisted of: a Site Agent, Ground-works Foreman, Foreman, Storeman and gangers (who would run the small gangs). The 'top dog' or 'big man' was the General Foreman and nobody would want to get in his bad books, he visited the site twice a week.

If the GF came to the site in the afternoon, he'd be pissed; if he came in the morning, he'd be still recovering from the night before! I'd say he was pissed 24 hours a day, his one-year old company car was a wreck, with new scrapes and dents all over the bloody thing. This was the culture at the time, everyone on site would have a few beers and drive home on a Friday night. Most of the Irish lads would have a few beers before heading off most nights. It was bloody hard work concreting, with the first few weeks leaving you with blisters and aching muscles. Working outside in all weathers would be the norm.

This particular day (being a Friday) Jim Casey, the General Foreman, was due to visit the site and take the managers to the pub at lunchtime. Outside our hoarding on the main road, the Gas Board were bringing in the new gas main to the site, it was a sunny warm day and the four gas workmen with the shovels were smoking – yes smoking in a trench working on the live gas! They said it was ok because they smoked roll ups – really? They were sitting having a break on the side of the trench, reading the Sun newspaper, drinking tea from a flask, when Casey turned up. He looked out of his car window and shouted at them to get on with their work, in his strong Irish accent.

They just looked at him and didn't move! He pulled over to the side, almost falling out of his car and like a raging bull he went out of the gates and onto the main road. He stood at the top of the trench and shouted, "You're all fired, get your stuff and get the fuck off my site, you lazy good for nothing wankers." He didn't have to tell them again, they just got up and left. No one wanted to tell him that he'd just sacked the Gas Board and they were nothing to do with us! He was in a very bad mood; he disappeared into the site office and then came out within a few minutes. He took two of the gangers for a pint; we were at the front of the site waiting for concrete.

We had a Wimpey yellow people carrier for the lads, it was parked up on site and in the back was a tall propane bottle, with a donkey jacket wrapped around it. From a distance, it did look like someone was in the back without a head! Casey came rolling out of the pub, smiling now, talking to everyone. "All right, ginger!" He used to call me the plastic paddy.

Casey was just about to fall into his car, when he spotted the gas bottle in the back of the van. He shouted out to Mick the Site Agent (who also was pissed as a fart), "Sack that fucking lazy waste of space" and pointed to the back of the van.

"It's a gas bottle," I said, but he looked at me and shouted, "get rid of him" (being me). As he drove past me, he opened his window to say something, but before he could say a word, he disappeared down the trench, exactly where the gas board had been working – good job he'd sent them home!

A JCB driver just drove around the rear of the car, put chains onto it and pulled him out. He put his hand out of the car window to say thanks to the driver and just drove off; he didn't even get out of the car. We knew if he sacked you when he was pissed, you could walk around the corner and come back and by then he'd have forgotten you. To be honest, this life was like being in a big playground for men. You always heard people joking and laughing on most sites, but always working hard.

Monday morning was for talking about the weekend football, by mid-week everyone was talking about the next weekend, always moaning about money and of course the weather. It was too cold, too hot or too wet.

I had now been working for Wimpey for about six months and most of the main concrete works had been completed. I had been made up to a Foreman, which meant more money and I managed a labour gang; we unloaded lorries and looked after the crane. I was in the Stores-Office, it was a wet morning and we had a delivery of 2000 bricks. A driver who was built like a brick shit house walked in, I was standing next to the store man who was about 5'6" and was a fiery Scot called Jock! This big lump of a driver had the hump, because he had been waiting for hours to get unloaded, and his voice boomed, "When am I getting unloaded?"

Jock said, "You'll have to wait."

The driver looked at him and said, "Pick a window, you're going out," and with that, Jock just launched himself at the tank!

It was so funny, chairs and desks went everywhere, punches were thrown, it was a frenzied attack. The driver was on the floor with the little

Jock head-butting him and punching him. I jumped in and pulled him off; but I got a punch in the head for my troubles! The driver just looked in shock, blood was running down his nose and he had a fat lip. It was over in seconds, as everyone came running in and for a few seconds it felt like time just stood still – like at the end of a boxing match. I was waiting for this lump to get up off the ground and eat Jock, but things went from bad to worse! He grabbed his chest. "Oh fuck me," he said, his face turned grey – he was having a heart attack in front of us. Back then, not many people had any first aid skills. I was lost, I didn't know what to do. Panicked looks on everyone's faces, when Jock kicked into action, he went right to work and just said "call 999". He said, "Hey pal, what's your name?"

"Ken."

"Bend your knees and let's sit you up against the wall. Get some water; do you take any pills, pal?"

"No."

This did not look good; he was clutching his chest.

"It's alright, pal."

Three of us just stood feeling so helpless, it's not a good feeling, you feel you should be doing something, but you can't. It seemed hours before the ambulance arrived at site. Jock (I use this name because he was only ever known as Jock, I never ever knew his real name), just kept him calm. "If you think this will get you unloaded first, you're right." Five minutes ago, they were trying to kill each other.

The ambulance lads got him up and loaded, with help from all of us – he must have been 25 stone! It's not like that now; they just had oxygen and wore a black uniform. He passed away later that day from a heart attack; he'd apparently had two before. The police interviewed Jock the day after and we never saw him again – he was sacked by Wimpey. Fights on site happened normally between drunk labourers and they fought anyone that looked the wrong way at them in the pub! It was a Friday and the end of the month Friday; this was a collection day for the lads back in Ireland – if you get my drift. I was in the pub on this day, due to the topping out of the site. Topping out is when the structure was finished and we left just a small square out, for one of the directors to put the last shovel of concrete in and float it off. It was a long tradition.

On top of the building were two beer barrels, for everyone to have a drink 'to the topping out' then all off to the local pub, where the money behind the bar was from Wimpey. Today in the pub a collection was going on, they only went to the Irish lads. But this time one of the lads on site was a Loyalist, so it kicked off with about 50 drunken men in the pub – it was a mass brawl. Someone called the police, three vans of them, SPG, Special Police Group (or Smash People Group).

They were notorious for their heavy-handed ways to say the least; they came bursting in with their truncheons out ready and started hitting out at everyone.

The lads gave back as good as they got, the police were getting thumped back, glasses and chairs flying; this went on for about five minutes. A gap opened up between the police and us, but I never took part in any of this, I just kept back. Then another van turned up with more officers, all over 6′ tall, the Sergeant just shouted, "calm down" and it seemed to be over.

Another sergeant came in and you could see he was itching for a fight. He just shouted, "You fucking Irish scum, fuck off back to paddy land, you murdering bastards."

Oh shit, this was fighting talk, it went mental, chairs and glasses started flying all over the place and I got hit over the head with a truncheon – my head opened like an egg, blood streamed down my face and he went to hit me again. I could hardly see through the blood in my eyes, I blocked his arm and threw him over my shoulder (due to being black belt Judo from school) and he landed on his arm, he broke his arm and let out this really loud shout of pain. His mates stopped and looked at him holding his arm, then focused on me; they jumped on me, were kicking me, punching me and it hurt so much that it did not hurt after a few seconds, I felt numb. Then it all fizzled out – I think. I wasn't sure how long it went on for, seconds maybe. I was dragged out by the scruff of my neck by three of them and they threw me into the back of the police van. Two officers got in with me, called me a 'Ginger Cunt', then they punched me in the ribs, even with hand cuffs on. Then in the face, they must have knocked me out for a few seconds – they hit me some more, but I don't remember it all. I know I looked like I'd been in the ring with two bare knuckle fighters.

I was taken to the 'Barking nick', thrown in a cell and left on a bench bed, bleeding for about an hour or so. I was dizzy and being sick, I had shit myself, wet myself and I couldn't see very well. I could only hear people moving, the sound of the peephole cover moving, as they looked in on me. I heard the door unlock and an Inspector came in. As soon as he saw me, he called for the Custody Officer. "Get this lad a doctor now – fucking now! What's your name, lad?"

"I don't know," I think I mumbled. I really could not remember. I could not speak properly; my lips were numb, and my jaw was not moving. I didn't know till later, that I was in a very bad way, when I was taken to hospital. It would have been easier to say which bit did not hurt!

I was in hospital for about 10 days; I thought I was only in hospital for about a day, I was so out of it. I had visitors from the Wimpey Construction lads, including the Regional Director.

My brothers came in to see me; they just got on with life at home – they never went to school of course! Wimpey paid my wages and gave them to Mickey for me.

I had two broken ribs, 12 stitches in my head and four in my right eye. I had bruises all over my body and I was due to be discharged. Before I left hospital, a Police Officer with scrambled egg on his shoulders (high ranking I think) walked up to my bed and pulled the curtains round. He sat down next me, he looked at me and said, "Son, it looks like we have a bit of a problem here, don't we?" I didn't say a word. "You hurt one of my officers, you broke his arm, you did that, and you could get up to five years for hitting an Officer. I am a reasonable man; it seems to me that you were attacked in the pub by others. We managed to get you out of there, to a safe place and my Officers tell me that they picked you up off the floor (for your own protection). Do you agree with that account of your injuries? Because – if you do, this will be the end of the matter. I am sorry, Stewart, for your injuries. Are we clear with the end of the matter then?"

I just nodded in agreement.

When I spoke to the doctor, he said it had been touch and go, as he thought I could have suffered a bleed on the brain. He said I'd been lucky it was just bruising. My respect for the law didn't change, I just thought I was in the wrong place at the wrong time (I think). I had visitors from the Wimpey site lads, all pissed after work, the paddies were a walking talking load and you could smell the beer in the hospital. They were all tanked up!

The Matron on the ward was also from Ireland, she clocked them or smelt them, and she bossed them around like a bunch of sheep. All they wanted to do was give me a donation from an anonymous person of £200. I later found out it was from Belfast in Ireland, but I never found out who actually gave it to me. I was back to work a few weeks later and the site had moved on a lot. I still looked a bit rough!

I was no longer the Foreman, as I'd been away, and the gang had gone to another site. I was now working with the Site Engineer for a few weeks, until I was fully recovered. I was told I had a meeting with the Regional Director, but I didn't know what for.

At home my brother had been busy, well Mick had, but Jerry just went along with life. From his brief encounter with the Children's Home, Mickey always made friends. He'd met two brothers, Darren and Walley, who had also been placed in the home.

The two of them were the most prolific thieves you would ever encounter, outside of Parkhurst Prison. If you wanted anything, they would find it and get it for you. Mickey said they needed a place to stay for a few days, so I agreed to five of us staying in the one bed flat! It was going to be tight but believe me when I say this will be eventful, it would be an understatement! First of all, I said they would have to pay their way, they asked if they could supply the food and I agreed.

The first night when I came home from work, I could not believe my eyes, we had a half a pig hanging from a large stainless-steel hook over the kitchen door. They'd nicked it from the back of a butcher's lorry, with the steel hook still in it! We also had chickens and loads of sausages in the fridge. I made a comment "all we need is eggs", and they both looked at each other and started shouting at each other. Darren said to his brother, "I told you to take the bloody eggs, you wanker," then they both started fighting and scrapping on the floor. They backed into the kitchen door, the half pig fell off the door and landed on one of them, pushing his head against the wall and it knocked him clean out. Darren must have been out for a few seconds and it took about a minute before he was able to focus. I was just stunned to see one of them, who had been dazed for a few minutes, starting to chop up the meat, as if nothing had happened! To make some money, we put meat in plastic bags and went around the building selling it on the cheap. We made a good 100 pounds and we lived like kings for a few weeks.

They both stayed for about three months and in this time, they were arrested three times for nicking car wheels from the back of the new Ford cars, which had been on the back of the trains inside Ford itself. Darren was the more prolific nutcase, he once nicked a police car and drove it around London for a night, with the lights going and everything (till it ran out of petrol) – they never got him for that. They then moved away to Manchester, as they had every Police Officer in the whole of London looking for them. We saw them from time to time, when they needed to hide for a few days. Last we heard, they were both doing very well in the world of chopped cars or ringing cars.

The time in the flat was different and we were building a very strong brotherly bond between us, almost unbreakable. We all just got on with life, having fun and just surviving. Jerry thought of himself as a practical joker – he was great at telling jokes, but useless at practical jokes.

I came home from work on this Saturday and Jerry and Mickey were in the bedroom. They called me in. As I was just about to walk through the door, I looked up to see a work boot balanced on top of the door, so I pushed it over the top. Jerry, who had placed the boot, was behind this door and the boot landed on his big toe and it broke it – he was jumping around all over the place! Mickey was rolling up with laughter and Jerry told him to shut up and chucked the boot at him – it hit him right on the top of the eye! Blood just spurted out everywhere, it was carnage. As I tried to get to Mickey to help him, I tripped on the other boot, put my hand out to save myself, but pushed Jerry over one of the beds. He was hopping on one leg and banged his head on the wall!

It couldn't get any worse, but it did. What I hadn't remembered was, I'd just got over a bout of gastroenteritis. I just shit myself, not just a little, my whole insides including my liver and kidneys came out too! It bloody stunk, so bad we just could not stop laughing, and the more I laughed the more it flowed out of me.

We as brothers became a strong family, a bit like 'the Trotters' in Only Fools and Horses, but we were a three. I had to throw away my clothes and then got a bus to the hospital with Jerry hopping along and Mickey holding his eye. We spent two hours in A&E, but it was all good. I still could smell shit; I needed a bath.

It was a time of our lives, everything went right for a few weeks, even Wimpey asked if I would like to become a trainee engineer. It would mean I would have to take a pay cut, spend six months on site and six months in college.

My football abilities had got me into the youth team of a well-known club, for three months. I am not giving their name, because years later they denied my existence – so fuck them – but to be frank the youth team they had, I was never going to break into it anyway. One of the coaches Ken said he had a friend at Dagenham FC (Ted Harding). I went along to see Ted, and the money was not bad for a Conference League team, but I got a better offer from Enfield Town. In hindsight, I should have gone with Ted Harding and Dagenham. It was my third game and an FA Cup game, on a very wet and cold October night. It was a hard-solid game, hard hitting and at half time we were up 1-0. I had the centre forward in my pocket.

We came out of the dressing room, mixing with the other players, when I overheard the opposition manager say to one of his players "take the ginger centre back out of the game". You would hear this all the time in the 70s, it was the norm. Ten minutes into the second half of the game, I was clearing the ball, standing on my right foot kicking with my left. A player slid in a foot high, his studs hit my knee and I took the full impact on my standing leg. Missing the ball completely, my leg just folded backwards. I don't remember much more, as the pain was so great. There was a crunching horrible sound, as my knee shattered, and my leg broke in two. The bone came through the back of my right leg.

I didn't know what to do, I was on the floor, but I didn't want to look down. One of the players shouted out to the St. John's ambulance team, while other players were trying to get hold of the player who did this to me – as a mass brawl kicked off!

I passed out for a short period I think; I woke up in the ambulance being sick. I was in real pain, this was before the good old paramedic; no drugs, no pain relief, or gas and air! I was taken in right away and I was met by an Aussie doctor. He was great, he just said, "Give him morphine now" – he saw the terrified look on my face – I really thought I'd lost my leg. They knocked me out and pinned my leg. Six months in plaster and it was the end of me playing football at any real standard ever again!

I couldn't work, so my team had a whip round and Wimpey construction came to my aid again. They put me in the stores and the drawing office on site – as long as I could get to site, I was good for work they said! I also was going to start training as an Engineer for them. I now had a car, but I couldn't drive it, to get me to work – this was a problem. Mickey was 15 and couldn't drive legally, but this was the 70s. . .

You could do anything and get away with it, so I gave him a crash course on how to drive the car. He was good, he picked it up in three lessons, he never hit anyone, he went up the curb a few times and almost ran over someone on the footpath when parking, but otherwise he managed ok. What he did was, drive me to the site using my car, parked it up and went on to school. Then he came back and took me home. However, he was a bad driver; it was fair to say my heart was in my mouth most of the time.

From this day forward, I stopped watching football and I didn't get involved for a very, very long time. I could not face the truth, and this was me being a bit of a coward. I couldn't face the horrible fact, that football wasn't going to be part of my ongoing life. I used the mind-set that someone is always worse off than me and that made me into a Jekyll & Hyde person inside. I also started at a local gym, to build strength in my leg after the plaster was taken off.

This Gym was only really for serious body builders, they were all big men and when I say big – all competition size. I managed to get in because I knew the brother of the owner (Keith Ruffle). His brother Martin also started the same time as I did. We'd worked together on site.

What I did not understand, was why this place was such a secret and exclusive – until about two months in, when a few of them started to talk with me. They all belonged to an East-end gang headed up by Mac; I will not give out any names as I promised!

The changing room was interesting; a few guys had handguns and items that would keep a small army happy! Most of them worked on the doors around Essex, London and Ilford.

As I was getting bigger and getting to know everyone, when I was fit, I was asked if I would like few nights work in Basildon, £150 per night cash only. I said yes. Mac the boss (who I'd only met once up till now) was a hard bastard, he'd been shot twice and stabbed so many times he was like a tea strainer. He carried a gun all the time. I'd kept away from all that, but the money would be good.

It was a Friday night and the gym was always empty, only a few people were around, most of the lads had gone or getting ready for night club working on the doors. This one lad always trained on his own, never said much, but he nodded to me most times I was in there.

On this particular Friday night, we'd both trained. When he'd finished training, I was almost finished. He left saying "night lads" and he went upstairs to the car park, it was about 10 pm. The car park was poorly lit as I came out, but I could see he was surrounded by four men shouting at him. As I got closer, they just rushed at him with baseball bats and bars! I dropped my kit bag and rushed in as well. We both got a pasting, but so did they. It must have lasted about 60 seconds, but it seemed longer. They ran off towards a dark transit van and sped off.

We both looked a mess; my hands were covered in blood and swollen. I had teeth impressions on my right knuckle and a cut to my head that was bleeding down the side of my face and dripping onto my yellow t-shirt. I hurt all over! He was in a bad way too. I helped him up off the floor, got him into my car and we both went to A&E. We spent a few hours getting stitched up, we spoke about what had happened and he just said, "sorry you got involved, mate". I said that I wasn't going to stand by and see you get a kicking. The doctor asked what had happened, but we just said we'd got into a punch up; he rolled his eyes and walked off shaking his head, as if he had seen more than enough of this scenario before. I took the lad home; our clothes were still covered in blood. His house in Chigwell had gates, with a Range Rover parked across the drive with two Gorillas sitting in it; believe it or not their names were Bill and Ben. I didn't know this at the time, so it's a retrospective comment. They didn't recognize my car as we pulled up in front of the gate; one of them got out and came over to look at us, then waved to his mate to move the car and open the gate. My window was down, Bill looked in, and said, "What happened to you, boss?" Pete said nothing, just looked hard at him. "Your dad is inside, so is your mother."

We pulled up outside the two black well polished doors, Pete got out first and said, "come in, mate". We walked in through to the hallway – the house was amazing! What hit me were the stairs in the hallway; a C shape, the floors were black and white tiles, with very high ceilings and they had eight bedrooms! I didn't get a tour of the house; I can only go on what I was told and what I saw.

Mac came through, took one look at us and blew up. "What the fucking hell happened, son?"

I was left standing in the hallway for a few minutes, while they went off to another room. Then Mac came back and said, "Thanks, son, go home now, mate."

"Alright." And he gave me two hundred in cash! "What's that for?"

"Just take it."

I got the feeling I had no choice. Me and Pete then become really good friends, talking all the time in the gym. We would go to many places in London, his family owned night clubs; we just had a lot of laughs.

This went on for about a year, just doing things. My weekends were taken up going out, always after the washing had been done with my brothers. I never got to see his family again; Pete really liked it that way. I really liked his sister, man, she was too old for me, but she was fantastic. She knew I liked her and played me like a fiddle! I remember the day all this came to an abrupt end; things at work were going well, my brothers had become more independent, Mickey had just left school and Jerry had another two years to go. Pete came to me and said, "Stew, I have to take over from my Dad, he is moving to Spain. Things are a little hot for him here, I need to ask you a question, mate. If we stay as good friends, you'll have to come and work for us and get to know the business, you will have a great life, lots of cash, never want for anything. Your brothers will have money too. It will be a change for you, because once I take over, other gangs are going to see you as a person who would be easy to get to against me."

I said no. I knew what his family were into and yes it would have been an easy life to start with, money was good, but I didn't want to be always looking over my shoulder.

Pete said, "You've been my best friend for the past year, it's been great and if you ever change your mind, come and find me."

Two weeks after the conversation with Pete, I had a knock at the flat door; it was Trevor (Pete's bodyguard or personal assistant if you like), he just put out his hand and gave me a set of car keys and a log book for a car. "Pete said enjoy it, mate, the white one downstairs. It's a year-old Zodiac, lovely car; it's yours."

"Why?"

"Because you are the boss's mate."

I went to the phone box and called him at his home. "Thanks for the car but why?"

"We have been mates and you've never treated me different, just a mate, not because of who I am. Plus you're an ugly fucker and you'll need all the help you can get to pull a few birds. Just don't sell it, drop it off to Jim Barking Scrap yard in a few years."

Pete then said to me, "I am going to give you another opportunity, to see if you would like to work for my family and we can meet later today; in your car at the place in Hackney."

The first thing I remember was the music of the Bee Gees playing, it was a nice pub, about 40 people were hanging around, a few women and lads talking. Pete called out to Bill, who I knew now a bit better – Ben had gone to Spain with Mac. (I still laugh to myself when I put those names together.) He came over. "Speak to Stew about what we do and what he will earn."

Bill in his former life was a bare knuckle fighter, about 5′10″ tall and the same width, he was very softly spoken, not what you would expect from his looks. He shook my hand. "Any friend of Pete's, you know"! He looked and winked at me. "You work for Pete's family you get no wages, just cash as it comes, and you'll never want for anything. We have a tailor, we get all our clobber from him at no cost to us and we get one of these–" he opened his jacket, and my eyes fixed on the holster with a black handled browning gun – "it's for our protection. We run errands, we collect money and if you get nicked, we have a brief on call. If you get banged up, or have to do some bird (prison), we take care of the family. Hold on a few minutes. . ." He walked off to talk to Pete, who was talking to two half dressed girls at the bar.

I could not hear the short conversation, but I was thinking Bill was getting permission to tell me something. I saw Pete nod, then Bill came back and said, "You would work with me, looking after the girls and taking them around to parties and places in London – keeping them safe! It's going to be long hours, very gratifying, lots of fun, with a little bit of agro thrown in from punters."

I was really tempted, I really was. The money, the power; I could see the attraction of this life and then the last thing he said was "the girls will always take care of your needs"!

I was a young man with hormones running all over the place!

Pete came back over to me and just said, "So what do you think, mate – fancy it?"

I said, "I don't know."

He smiled at me with a glint of disappointment. "Come on mate, let's go. Pete walked with me, back to the car he gave me. I just started to get into the car when he said, "Stew mate, I am off to Spain for a few weeks with the old man, this will be the last time I see you."

"Why? I have not said yes or no yet."

"Stew, you are my best friend, why the fuck would I want you to work for me; you would not be my friend anymore."

"No?"

"Best this way, mate, you get me?" Pete put out his hand to shake mine, but as I went to shake it, he pulled it away and did that thing of, thumb on the nose wiggling his fingers. He walked towards me, put up his arms and hugged me.

"Be safe, Stew and if you ever need me, just call me." He walked off; Bill was still standing on the corner waiting for him. To this day, I have never seen him again. Bill, on the other hand, I did for about six months – he would come around just to see if everything was good (sent by Pete). After about six months, Bill stopped me by the car and said, "Mate, I am off now, it's safe now."

"Now?"

"Well, another gang found out that you were Pete's friend and the boss was worried they were going to find you and hurt you, it's all sorted now." Bill patted me on the shoulder, turned, got in his car and drove off – never to be seen by me again.

The time in the flat had passed quickly, Jerry was the boy whiz kid, Mickey had got himself a job as a trainee printer in central London, Fleet Street. Mickey had managed to get Jerry a summer job helping him. Jerry was now 15 and was in his last year at School and I had finished at Wimpey in Dagenham and had been moved to a new site 'Gardeners Corner' in Aldgate East. This was a new development of offices and a basement three storeys below ground. Me and my brothers would travel up together on the District line train. Mickey was the biggest piss taker you could ever meet in your life. If anyone had a personal defect, he would spot it a mile away.

We were all on this packed train and Mickey could smell a really horrible fart in the air.

My brain was not quick enough (like his), I was just about to say, "Mick you stink", but Mick got in first! In a very loud voice and waving his hands in front of his face he said, "Stew mate, that's disgusting, you stink, that's horrible."

Jerry just got off the train, because he could not hold in his laughter and embarrassment. I was lost for words, went red and started to laugh.

Mickey started to wave his paper, to woof it away and the space around me started to open up! I could not stop laughing as Mick kept up the abuse; he said, "Brov, you need help with that"! I had to get off the train, I didn't have time to feel embarrassed, I could not breathe! When I got off the train and the doors closing behind me, there was my shit bag of a brother, grinning like a Cheshire Cat, as the train moved off.

So, Jerry and I needed to get him back, but every time we tried, he was too quick for us. Jerry gave up, he just would not sit next to us – he'd had enough! Mickey made us laugh so much, Jerry would just sit down and make out he was asleep. That was until Mickey noticed that the glass was missing where Jerry was sitting (where people would stand or lean), it was next to the opening doors and when the train got packed people would lean against it, they had no choice when it was packed like sardines. Someone from the underground had placed yellow and black tape in the gap, but when Jerry fell asleep, Mickey took the tape away. When we got on the train at Dagenham it was never very full, till it got to Mile End.

This woman got on the train with her suitcase, then she turned her back to lean against the missing glass, she went straight through and landed on Jerry's lap! Her legs and arms went flying everywhere, Jerry just looked in amazement at this woman flailing around, trying to right herself. Mickey just ripped Jerry; it was so, so funny. After that, Jerry never travelled on the same carriage as Mickey again (anyway, Mickey used to get fed up with Jerry). Mickey would eat a Mars Bar in a few bites and Jerry would make his last for about 30 minutes – it would drive Mickey mad, and me to be fair, Jerry just nibbled his. Jerry did get Mickey back, only once as far as I know.

We had stopped at Whitechapel station; the signals weren't working, so we stood for about 10 minutes. Jerry told Mickey that the train on the other platform was about to go first and it had spare seats on it. Jerry got off the train, as if to head across the platform to get on the other train, Mickey seeing the seats, went past Jerry and jumped on the train. Jerry turned back, just as the doors were closing on our train and we went off! Mickey's train went the other way, he was really pissed, he was over an hour late getting to work after that.

I was one of the site engineers at Wimpey now at Gardeners Corner. Our project manager was a dead ringer for Mr Fawlty or Basil from Fawlty Towers. Jerry had left school now, so I managed to get him a job working on the wall breaking gang. It was a very well-paid job, but bloody hard on the hands. Using heavy hand breakers all day long, shook you to the very bone. Simon Short was the Project Manager's name, did well at his job and he was a bit of a headmaster type, if you get my meaning. I became a bit of a practical joker, back in the late 70s, early 80s, building sites were not the safest place to work, it was hard work, but good fun to work on site at that time.

My first practical joke was set up in the site toilets, they were thunder boxes, mostly for the piling team and the first groundworkers, till we had established the drains. Now some people call them portaloos, and these are a box made of wood or tin, with a door and a chemical bucket inside. At the end of every day, the labourer would have to get a hole dug and tip it in, or down the main drains. The worst days were when the thunder boxes were full, either a Monday morning or a Friday afternoon. I didn't know the reason for this, but they just were.

I never used them at all, but the site excavator drivers and piling teams did. I did this, to a lad who always read his Sun, whilst having a tom tit in this particular tin shitter. He was such a grumpy git! I placed underneath the box, a 4-inch water main hose which I attached to the hydrant outside in the street. I let him settle in, then I placed a wooden wedge outside his door, before I told one of the lads to open up. Bloody hell, this was fantastic, he just blew up, shouting and calling us all the names you could think of and more!

There was water coming out of the roof and the floor, he was kicking the door, shouting "you are fucking wankers, I'll kill you all". We all ran off, shut off the water and he managed to get out. If he found out who did it – my god! He was standing there, jeans halfway down, completely drenched, with steam coming out of his ears. He stormed off, went home and we lost a driver for the day. Oops, I got that in the neck and Simon seemed to know it was me! They got me back, I should have seen it coming.

It was late on a Friday, a concrete pour was running all night, 600 metres of the stuff for the main basement slab. As we were 70 feet below ground level, they would lower a thunder box down for the lads to use, instead of going up and down the scaffolding stairs. We lowered the thunder box down, using the mobile crane, which sat on a ply board, on top of the steel. I was in charge of the pour, as the engineer. I was with Nick the steel fixer boss, who was watching the work going on, under floodlights, we were waiting for the next load of concrete. I really was busting for a pee, but I could not leave the pour.

I said, "Nick, can you watch out for next load, mate?"

"Yep – no worries."

As soon as I got in, the door slammed behind me and one of the men locked the door from outside. From all over the site, bloody men started to bang the sides of this tin shitter, it was deafening. It was bad even holding my hands over my ears! I looked down and noticed that the bucket was totally full of shit, blue chemicals and bog paper. I knew at that moment, it would only be time before it was tipped over. The box was hooked up on the crane, lifted up to ground level and then flipped over on its side! I had no chance. I had toilet roll and shit in places I never thought possible. In my eyes, ears, mouth and hair – I stunk! I crawled out, to see about 30 lads having a good old laugh at my expense. I went home on the train stinking, wearing yellow waterproofs and wellies (nothing on underneath). I was not leaving it at that, it just got worse. It became a competition between us all – lads had their boots nailed to the ceiling, crap in their boots, cling film on the bogs. It got so bad, that the project manager finally had a meeting in the canteen to tell us it had to stop, and it did for a little while.

It was a Monday morning; I'd just got to work when I came across a full-size male mannequin! We had some fun with it, dressed it in all sorts of stuff, from dresses to batman, even a fire-fighter. It was just sitting around on site. It was fun for a few days, but it was then time to step it up!

A few of us were up on the 5th floor, me and a few of the other managers (including Jerry, who now worked for a stone company and was on site as a trainee Stone Mason). We were thinking of what to do with 'Del the mannequin' putting him in different silly poses? It was about 5pm and people were going home from work and standing at the bus stop. I looked at the queue of people, they were mostly women (the mannequin was wearing a blue boiler suit at the time). Jerry was holding it, I grabbed it off Jerry and started shouting at it, I said very loudly, so the people could hear me at the bus stop: "I told you to fuck off my site, you are sacked." I could see from the corner of my eye people looking up, so I did no more then throw him off the building! As I looked over, as it headed towards the ground I shouted, "I bloody told you to fuck off." People just started screaming, one woman fainted and the rest of the lads who were with me ran off.

About 20 minutes later, police and an ambulance turned up; I got loads of messages coming across my radio – "Stewart, can you get to the office now please."

These two coppers, or Old Bill, plus an ambulance woman were waiting with Simon.

"There's been a report of a fight and a person being pushed off the building (according to the officers)."

"No, not a clue what you are talking about."

"Come on, Stewart – what happened?"

"I just tossed the mannequin off the building, I thought it was funny."

The police did see the funny side of it, but Simon didn't, so I got a real bollocking.

A few weeks later I found the same mannequin. It was late, so for a bit of fun I found a saw and cut the neck and leant it to one side. I then got a rope, tied a hangman's knot and attached it to a scaffold tube. I'd dressed it in a boiler suit and added a helmet. I slid it out over the site, but as it was dark, it couldn't really be seen. The following morning, as I was walking towards the site from the station, I could see the fantastically real looking man hanging! To my surprise, the Police, Fire Service and Ambulance were all in attendance. Man – was I going to be in some trouble! That was for sure, I got transferred to the News International site for a few weeks as a punishment. I did return back, thank god; the other site was on strike every other day.

Simon Short was one of those people everyone would look at and say, you are a genuine person – he just was a very likable person. He was going to be a Director of Wimpey one day and we all knew that. It was so good to meet and work with this nice human being. These were the good times, when Construction companies looked after their staff, but safety was not very good. The big companies seemed to share the work around, so you would always come across people you had worked with in the past. Small world!

Strikes – well, the construction industry was going through a transition, and health and safety was the biggest reason for this. The companies were not happy with the cost and the changes, which resulted in all clashes between the unions and the management. We lost one man on site due to a health and safety issue – the scaffold slipped, and he fell 50 feet without a harness. There were many head injuries and with no guards on tools, many fingers lost. In the 70s and 80s, a blacklist did exist, even though the companies said it didn't. We all knew it did and every man who was in the union knew.

My stay at News International was short, due to my views on the way the Union was dealing with things. Don't get me wrong, I am totally for unions; they saved the industry from itself and helped countless people. We forget what they did for the common person. Yes – some unions became too powerful and cut off their nose to spite their face and this was the case at News International. I was on site for one day and a strike was called because the canteen was closed due to sickness. The company never made provision for this, so we had a mass walk out!

It was sad and I said in the union meeting, "we could work with management and get hot water for tea and let them sort the rest".

"No, fuck them."

We all walked out for the day; this was what it had got too.

The unions didn't give an inch, nor did management. For the three weeks I was on site, I prevented two strikes by talking to contractors who were fed up to the back teeth. The Union didn't like this, and I was sent back to the Aldgate site.

Simon said, "Are you able to stop being silly now?"

"No, I will always be silly, you know that."

He smiled. "Get out, Stewart, you will be the death of me. Stewart, you are in charge of health and safety as well now."

Our site was held up as a top safety site in London, when we had the HSE come to inspect us. I was asked to take the health and safety officer around site externally. We were walking along the external scaffolding five floors up; we were talking as we walked. All of a sudden, he disappeared through the scaffold boards. My god, he was gone! He was lying on the lift below, shook up, not hurt but a little shocked.

I called on the radio for urgent assistance from other managers who came quickly. Nothing seemed wrong with him, when we got him inside the building. Simon appeared very quickly and came over to us with the other health and safety people. He looked at me like I had killed him.

"What bloody happened?"

I explained. I'm sure he thought I'd done something – well, could you blame him! The site was closed down for the rest of the day. Nearly killing a member of the HSE was not very good.

On inspection, the scaffolding boards had knots in them and one of them had given way – this was a major problem! The whole site had to have all the boards changed, before the site could restart and it added three weeks to the program. Funnily enough, we lost our best site record! We had a few more incidents on site – one was when two lads were lifting ply boards up and clearing them from the site to the skips. They did this by picking up one end and walking their hands along – till they got to the middle of a 4′ to 8′ sheet, then lifted it over their heads and walked off with them. I and three other managers were doing our walk round and two labourers were clearing shuttering. One lad picked up a board and started to walk it (without looking) and then he was gone! The board slammed down as if it was a lid and he fell two floors and bounced off the boards that were covering the same hole two floors below. This hole was 600 × 600 and went all the way through the building. How he fitted through the next floor without hitting the sides was a small wonder. Mind you, he was a thin lad; his mate wouldn't have fit, he was a big lump! Not a scratch – he just came back up and got on with his work, as if nothing had happened or it was the norm for him. Again, this changed health and safety and from now on all holes on site (if covered by ply) had to be fixed down or fenced off.

Health and safety on sites was coming of age and one of the biggest things was First Aid. It was hit and miss on sites, most site teams never knew much; the First Aid box was always in the stores or the office. The store man was the 'go to man' for help, as we hoped he knew how to put a plaster on. My views on this as assistant construction manager were brought into reality and I felt we should have a trained First Aid person.

One evening, we had a concrete pour on the upper floors, we had to crane in the concrete using a concrete skip and this big yellow skip had a spring-loaded chute. As the crane lifts it to the location, we would release the chute and let the concrete pour slowly into shuttering. A good crane driver would work with you, because a cubic metre of concrete weighs about a tonne and as the weight reduced, the crane would start to lift the Jib. The driver would slack off the cable, to compensate for the movement up and down.

On this particular day it was raining heavily and we had a new crane driver. I was standing behind two men holding the skip in place loaded with concrete. We were five floors up. The first labourer opened the skip too fast, this then had a knock-on effect to the crane, the driver didn't compensate quick enough, so it shot up in the air! The driver then dropped the skip down, causing the skip to bounce, hitting the first labourer, who then fell backwards onto me! The scaffolding system we used on the site was a clip and wedge system, yellow in colour; if you're old enough, you will know the system. It was removed from use some years later. It pushed me through the safety rail, that had not had the wedge placed correctly and all I can remember was thinking "this is it". I must have blacked out, I don't remember hitting the sand pits below, over a 60′ drop. The most ironic thing was, I am the one who had the sand pits moved to that location. I didn't know if I was dead or not! I woke up three days later in hospital. I was in so much pain, I couldn't move, I had two broken legs, six broken ribs, a broken collarbone and a fractured skull. All in all, I was in a good place – alive!

My brothers came up to see me – they just took the piss out of me! Mickey called me the Kit Kat Kid – "Have a break". Jerry just drew pictures on my head when I was asleep, and the nurses had to keep wiping them off. Wimpey paid my wages to Mickey; he went to site to collect them every week and Simon Short (the project manager) would come to see me every few days. No claiming back then, you were just lucky that you never got sacked for almost killing yourself! I was in hospital for about six weeks in total.

One of the nurses took a shine to me and we talked a lot when she was on nights. It was about five weeks in and I was about to start to walk on crutches. She also gave me a bed bath and that was the hardest thing I had ever experienced. I was in pain all over and she would wash every part of me – it was hard not to jump when she washed my private parts! She was a short young Irish girl called Morgan; she was slim with black hair.

Morgan was a black Irish girl. She told me her dad was white and from London and her mum was from Jamaica. She planned to work out in Jamaica for a few years, to help her grandfather run a small hospital. One day she asked if I'd like to walk to the next ward, as it was empty, and it would help me more. When I finally got around to the overflow ward, it was not very well lit. Morgan said, "Come on then, let's get you walking better, no one is watching here."

We always had a good laugh about my bad luck, then she told me that she was leaving the hospital and was going to Jamaica very soon.

I said, "That's sad, will you miss me?"

She said, "of course" with a little grin on her face and without warning she just blurted out "have sex with me".

Believe me, she did not have to ask again before I could say "when". I had an erection sticking out the front of my hospital trousers. She eased me across to one of the empty beds, she sat me down on the bed and lifted her uniform. She straddled me and moved her knickers to one side sliding me inside her! The pain was bad, my body was in a mix of pain and pleasure, not a good combination and she only lasted a few seconds. Thank God, the pain was so great. My body was not ready for this, I couldn't stay hard for long. She kissed me and helped me back to my ward and my bed.

She was leaving in five days and she was on nights all week. When they gave you a bed bath, they always drew the curtains. This particular night, she walked in and whispered in my ear, "Time for a bed bath, Stewart, you need to rest after all the walking around the ward, let me do the work." She just gave me this fantastic wash, it was so nice and erotic. Morgan would always go around, making sure everyone in the ward was sorted for the night before coming to me.

My bed was moved into the corner, with 14 beds in the ward and there were only six of us. It was a pain for me, I was right at one end of the ward and the other lads or older men were at other end – say about 20 feet away. Lights would usually go out at about 10 pm. This night she kissed me and got hold of my good hand and put it up her dress. We almost got caught – one of the sisters came around and opened up the screen, my hand was up the front of her uniform and she had just started to climax.

"Nurse?"

"Yes, Sister?"

She was standing right behind Morgan – if she had come around the front, I don't know what she would have said.

"Hurry up, the doctor will be here soon."

Sister just closed the screen and walked off. Morgan gripped my arm so hard, she left nail marks. She said that was so intense. I never even got her full name; she was gone, and I never saw her again – ever. I asked the other nurses, and they said she had gone to her Jamaican family.

I did get better quicker, I know that. I was back at a desk 10 weeks later, still with a walking stick and plaster only on one leg. I must say Wimpey

Construction knew how to look after their staff. The amount of times Wimpey looked after me must been a record!

The project was coming to an end; life was still good for me and now feeling better, being my usual nutty self. Wimpey offered me a new project of my own, in East London (a new Texas store to construct). This was going to be different, my first Site Agent project. Life at home was ok, Mickey had found himself a girlfriend called Liz, and Jerry was leaving in a few months to go and work in Israel on a working farm for a year. I was still single and happy with my lot so to speak.

The flat was looking good, I had a really nice car (a Capri 1.6), I had a few pounds in my pocket – most of the time anyway!

IN CONCLUSION

I HAVE REALLY BEEN TO HELL AND BACK, more than once. I am so used to it; I have a clearly worn path. I have experienced highs and lows that can't be explained – maybe if I had a crystal ball with me at all times. I wander through this life, taking everything it wants to throw at me and sometimes I feel like the human equivalent of the Titanic – it's just taking a bit longer to sink me!

I have lived my life and survived this jungle of humanity, without ever blaming anyone for my situation. I have no right to say I have suffered, for all over the world my pain is nothing compared to the mothers, fathers, sisters and brothers of the Manchester bombings, or the war-torn countries. Parents who watch their families die from hunger. This is why I can never feel my life has been horrific. Yes, I do feel sad for myself sometimes, it depends how long I want to wallow in self-pity.

I have so much more to tell the world, yet I feel now is the point to end this chapter of my life.

I will continue to write and live my continuing chapter of life. I have come of age, my sharpness, wits and ability to survive have become more acute.

Hold onto your hats, the story of my life continues, and I hope you will join me in the future. I hope you will enjoy the fun, the intrigue and the downright bullshit – it will blow your mind! From sadness and pain that will bring you to the belief that I may be telling you lies. Rest assured, it will be the truth.

My path from this date on has been one of wonder, becoming a Police Officer, Fire officer, a bad businessman and saving lives. Being proud, playing for my country and Chelsea Legends. Lost loved ones, meeting real friends, Nicolas, Karen, Jan, Phil and my children. Many people have changed the direction of my life and Reggie my dog, who saved me from a very dark place.

I have written this book with my heart and soul, but the names have been changed to protect the people – it's only fair.

Thank you for coming into my small world of humanity, in its full glory!

Printed in Great Britain
by Amazon

37648522R00099